Transformation of the HEART

This wonderful book is a collection of stories by people whose lives have been transformed by Sathya Sai Baba. Written with warmth and compassion, these stories provide a unique and personal glimpse of Sai Baba, one of the most impressive men of miracles to appear for centuries. Sathya Sai Baba has millions of followers in India, as well as in many countries around the world. He amazes people with his wisdom, knowledge, power and unconditional love. These personal narratives, written by people who share our normal, everyday lives, show how true spiritual awakening occurs under vastly different circumstances, outlooks, educations, backgrounds, and philosophical approaches to life. This is an important book to help people understand the message of Sathya Sai Baba, the Avatar of our age.

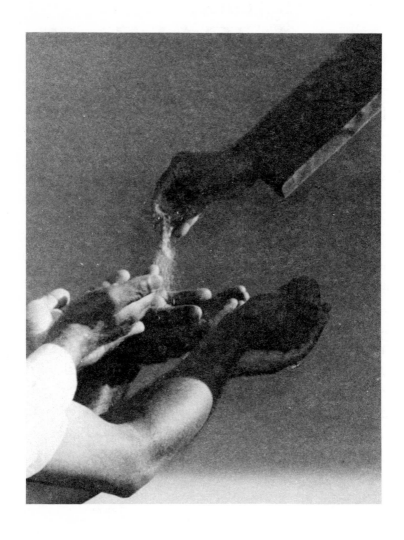

Sathya Sai Baba creating vibhuti.

Transformation of the HEART

Stories by Devotees of
Sathya Sai Baba

Compiled and edited by Judy Warner

SAMUEL WEISER, INC.
York Beach, Maine

First published in 1990 by
Samuel Weiser, Inc.
Box 612
York Beach, Maine 03910

Library of Congress Cataloging-in-Publication Data

Transformation of the heart: stories by devotees of Sathya Sai
Baba /
    compiled and edited by Judy Warner.
    1. Sathya Sai Baba, 1926-   I. Warner, Judy.

BL1175.S385T72 1990   90-77667
294.5'092—dc20   CIP
ISBN 0-87728-716-3

Text illustrations © Kazuko Chuma, 1990; front cover photograph
© David Wolff, 1990; backcover photograph and frontispiece
© Padmanabhan, 1990.

Typeset in 11 point Goudy
Printed in the United States of America by
Baker Johnson, Inc.

Dedicated
with love and devotion
to
Bhagavan Sri Sathya Sai Baba

CONTENTS

Acknowledgments ix

Introduction xi

Can God Hear Me?
Jack Scher 1

An Extraordinary Journey
Barbara Bozzani 19

Seeking Love
Bea Flaig 33

It's All God
Allen S. Levy 43

Letting Go Is Letting God In
Judy Warner 53

Descending of the Holy Spirit
Pauline Kirby 77

In This Lifetime
Dorothy Herron 89

Turning Inward
Hugh Brecher 99

The Eclipse
Mimi Goldberg 115

Near and Dear
Rosie Loew 123

Sweet Sai Sweet Self
Al Drucker 135

Unity is Divinity
Mary Lynn Radford 157

Glossary 175

Bibliography 181

ACKNOWLEDGMENTS

I would like to express my gratitude to:

Mary Lynn Radford for her help in copyediting this book, as well as for her additional help with creative editing.

Warren White for his help with word processing and valuable layout and design suggestions.

Kazuko Chuma for her original drawings.

David Wolff for his front cover photograph; Padmanabhan for his back cover photograph and frontispiece photograph.

Barbara Bozzani, editor of the *Sathya Sai Newsletter* for allowing some of the authors to build on stories that originally appeared there.

Sathya Sai Baba. Without his grace, none of these stories would have been written nor would this book have been published.

INTRODUCTION

This book is intended for two groups of readers: those who already know of Sathya Sai Baba, and those who are still searching and have come upon this book "by accident."

Sathyanarayana Raju, as Sai Baba was named, was born on November 23, 1926, in the village of Puttaparthi, India, where his ashram now stands. He came into the world with all knowledge, wisdom, power and divine love. Unlike self-realized saints, he did not have to practice disciplines or austerities to achieve his divinity.

Although Sai Baba only attended school to the age of thirteen, he has complete mastery of the scriptures, of all the sciences, arts, languages—of all fields of study. As a matter of fact, he knows everything—including the past, present and future of all of our lives.

Sathya Sai Baba has millions of followers in India, as well as in many countries around the world. He has incarnated at this time to restore truth, righteousness, peace and love in the world and to transform all our hearts so that we can experience that we, too, are divine.

For a full account of Sai Baba's life, see N. Kasturi's biography entitled *Sathyam, Sivam Sundaram* and other titles listed in the Bibliography.

How I have yearned to present this manuscript to Baba. On January 3, 1989, my dream came true. There I was, manuscript in hand, sitting at the lotus feet of my beloved guru when he turned and asked, "What is that?"

"Your book, Swami," I replied as I handed him the manuscript.

He looked at the cover and the first few pages and said, "What is the title?"

"Transformation of the Heart."

With a smile he asked, "Which heart is that—spiritual heart or physical heart?"

"I hope spiritual heart, Swami."

"Good," he said with a twinkle in his eye. "The only transformation of the physical heart is bypass." Everyone laughed as he reached for my pen to lovingly sign this manuscript. A long awaited prayer had, once again, been fulfilled.

The stories in this book are but a few examples of what happens when Sai Baba touches our lives. These are all stories with happy endings, or, perhaps, happy beginnings. May Sai Baba reach out through these pages and touch you, bringing love and joy into your lives.

JW

TRANSFORMATION
OF
THE HEART

Stories by devotees

of

Sathya Sai Baba

Compiled & Edited

by

Judy Warner

It is not enough to calculate the amount of your sadhana or the hours you spend in study or meditation. The Lord comes more for the Transformation of your heart into a reservoir of Love. He does not count the recitations and adoration you offer as more valuable. The heart filled with compassion is the temple in which He likes to install Himself.

—Sathya Sai Baba

CAN GOD HEAR ME?

Jack Scher

When I was a little boy they told me, "Be good or God will punish you; God is watching you all the time. He can see everything you do; you can't hide from him." They told me he looked like a man, but you couldn't see him. I thought he had to be very large, big enough to see everyone on earth, very strong to be so powerful because he could do anything, and very old to be so wise.

They said, "Close your eyes and pray to him." So I got the idea that it really wasn't important to see him. It seemed as if praying was like making a big or very special wish. First, you had to ask for forgiveness; you had to say you were sorry for all the bad things you had done. I would name the few that I remembered, and then ask for forgiveness for all my other sins.

The good part about praying was being able to ask for anything that you wanted. I would lie in my bed and think about all the things I would like to have and then ask for them. If there was something I wanted more than anything else, I would get down on my knees and clasp my hands together. I wasn't even very disappointed when nothing seemed to happen; I would just continue to hope and pray and ask for more.

Somewhere I got the idea that asking for things just for myself was wrong. So I would pray to God to bless my mother, my father, and the whole family. In that way I was included. I went on like this for years. Praying became something I had to do before sleep. I had to do it just in case it might work and also to protect myself if there really was a God watching.

My father was an orthodox Jew. He took me to the local shul where the women sat upstairs. The men sat below with their little black skull caps and silk striped tallithim. They rocked back and forth, moaning their prayers in some low, foreign, rhythmic cadence. There was nothing I could understand, but

I knew it was important to be in the temple, just like making sure to say my prayers each night.

My father died suddenly when I was 5. Many men came to the house to say kaddish. I was given a book, a skull cap and tallith, told to face east and pray: *Shma Yisroel Adaunai Eloheynu* . . . Repeating the magic words I thought something special might happen; but God did not come, nor did my father.

Three years later my mother remarried and was paralyzed by polio. My stepfather was a Christian Scientist, and he believed it would help my mother if I went to his church. Here they taught me about Mary Baker Eddy and the Ten Commandments and how to sing "Onward Christian Soldiers." My mother had a Christian Science nurse plus a little old lady dressed in black who would come to the house to read the Bible to her. But their prayers were never answered. My mother remained paralyzed from the waist down until her death twenty years later.

My Aunt Bertha was a potential source of spiritual guidance. She had a doctorate in philosophy and lectured coast to coast about the "Oneness of God." She had a large following during the 1930's, particularly among women's groups. She wrote a number of books. I remember one called *Joseph, He Has Never Left Us*. It was dedicated to my father, her brother. The cover had a picture of a naked man crouching in the distance with a spiral of smoke rising from the top of his head and going up into the sky. My parents thought she was crazy, and I was forbidden to see her because she made it clear that she didn't approve of my mother's new marriage. I continued to meet her in secret because she was the only person I had ever known who loved me unconditionally. However, I never was interested in, or followed, her teachings.

I grew up then without any real concern or belief in God. When I got to college I was briefly interested in understanding how the world began. There were three basic arguments or propositions:

1. The world always was, and always will be.

This was impossible. Surely there must have been a time before the world began.

2. The world started itself, and it is finite or it goes
on forever.

This was also impossible. The world had to start itself with something, and where did that "something" come from?

3. The world was started by an outside source,
probably divine and therefore unknowable.

Another impossibility. If God started the world, where did he come from? Who or what started him?

I learned that when you have several arguments of equal impossibility, you use Occum's law of the razor. You choose the simplest. I was never satisfied with the concept that the world always was, nor was I happy with a belief in a God whose existence was impossible to prove and depended entirely upon blind faith!

By the time I graduated from college, all thoughts of God had receded to an unconscious level. Perhaps because of this loss, I had an overwhelming fear of dying. Without God, my death meant total obliteration. The idea that I would never breathe, feel, see, touch—or more importantly, know myself again, consumed me with an unrelenting fear that fed on itself. No one else seemed to have my degree of concern. Yes, they knew in the end they would die and that there would be nothing left, but since there isn't anything that you can do about it, you might as well forget it and concentrate on the present.

I remember lines from a poem by Walter Benton:

Because our day is of time, of hours—and the clock-
hand turns, closes the circle upon us: and black time-
less night sucks us in like quicksand, receives us

totally—without a raincheck or a parachute, a key to
heaven or the last long look . . .[1]

Psychotherapy didn't help. The therapist said my fear was due to the fact that I wasn't getting enough out of life, that the fear would go when I became more involved in living. Then there wouldn't be any time to think about dying.

The best consolation my psychiatrist could offer were the tales of the Kalahari. This nomadic African tribe is constantly on the move. When their people get too old to travel, they voluntarily stay behind knowing they face certain death from starvation. As the old people sit and wait to die, they somehow make their peace with this earth life . . . and their eyes turn blue like the sky above them.

I tried to accept that we are here for just one brief moment. My goal was to live each day fully, try to be happy and, above all, make a lot of money. My fear of death took a back seat. It only surfaced when I was sick, had a pain of unknown origin, or learned that someone I knew had died.

Within twelve years I had become one of the best paid medical advertising space salesmen. I was married and had three children. At age 39 I decided to quit my lucrative job and try to become a publisher. Life seemed too short to live and die just to make money. The whole experience was like a dream; one successful medical newspaper followed another; I was listed in *Who's Who*, and became a millionaire. My only problem was I still didn't believe in myself. It took years of psychoanalysis to finally accept that I hadn't fooled anyone, that I won because I worked hard and was good at what I did.

When I was 19 I promised myself that if I ever really made it in this world, I wouldn't hang in there trying to have more money or more success. Instead, I would quit and enjoy it. At age 49 I sold the company and was completely free to do anything I wanted.

---

[1] Walter Benton, *This Is My Beloved* (New York: Knopf, 1943).

In 1976, five years after my divorce, I met Judy, the woman who is the love of my life. For seven years we played at discovering what the world has to offer. I thought I was very happy, but I was drinking too much, and smoking too much marijuana. I left New York, built a beautiful geodesic dome in Virginia, and started doing research in parapsychology. I thought I had everything I needed except, perhaps, eternal life!

I took several courses at the Monroe Institute in an attempt to have an "out of the body" experience. If I could only get out, this would prove that I was more than my physical body. I didn't make it; but somehow in the process, I started to be more open. I realized the only way I could continue to grow was to suspend judgment; and the people who did get out seemed to have similar experiences: Love is the answer to everything, and we are energy personalities incarnating for the purpose of growth and exploration. A whole series of synchronistic events began to disassemble and restructure my belief systems. Reading Seth, reports of near death experiences, chance meetings with healers, channels, people with spiritual guides—I was surrounded and I liked it.

I first heard about Sai Baba from a friend who is a psychic healer. She had several of his pictures around the house. She said he was her Master. I never asked her any questions. Another time she gave a dinner party where I met a man who had just returned from Baba's ashram. Again, I didn't even ask who he was. Clearly I wasn't ready. They say the only people who come to Baba are those whom he has called.

In October 1984, Judy and I picked up two Baba books: *Sai Baba, The Holy Man and the Psychiatrist*, by Sam Sandweiss, and *Avatar*, by Howard Murphet. We were both more than enthusiastic to make India our next trip. Judy, while happy with her life, yearned to feel connected to the God force. I liked the descriptions of Baba's Christ-like existence and the miracles. My casual thought was if someone like Jesus was really alive and walking the earth, then what could be better than checking him out.

I felt some trepidation before we left. I loved what I had read about Baba, but he had so many rules: "Do Good, See Good, Be Good"; "Work is Worship"; "Duty, Devotion . . ." I kept finding it difficult to remember the word "Discipline"! I was afraid; I really didn't think Baba was God, but suppose he was and he captured me? I'd have to do all those things . . . "Watch my Words, my Actions, my Deeds." My whole life would change.

Just before we left, I saw Baba in a dream. He looked at me very sternly, and in a deep voice said, "What do you want?" I said that I wanted to know that death is not the end and that I will have a continuing awareness of myself after death.

To say that life in Baba's ashram is austere reflects a newly found gentleness in my thinking. I was angry, hopeful, disappointed, fascinated, and sometimes very lonely. Most of all I wanted a personal interview. I longed for Baba to tell me things about myself that would prove to me that he was God. Each day, twice a day, I would line up and wait. Whenever I was lucky enough to sit in the first row, my fatigue fell away and the trees seemed to sway and dance in the breeze. Baba would come so close I could reach out and touch him, but he never even looked at me. I watched as eager devotees grabbed at his footprints in the sand, joyfully throwing the holy sand on their hair, heads and children; and some, even eating it. What did I have to lose? I sprinkled some on my head too.

Judy tried unsuccessfully to be helpful. "Baba knows what is best; perhaps you just aren't ready for an interview." This kind of talk was infuriating. Everyone always had positive answers as to why things didn't go the way I wanted.

I saw the Australians with their green and white scarves, the Argentines all dressed in pale green, the Nepalese all wearing their funny little hats. It seemed that groups had the best chance for an interview. We even considered forming a group of lone Americans.

I tried the mandir. The vibrational sounds from the bhajans are supposed to transport and nourish the soul. Instead, I sat there all scrunched up, knees and bodies prodding me from every direction. The walls were lined with statues of animals and pagan looking gods, huge life-size pictures of Baba and Shirdi Baba framed in gold looking down at us, and hanging overhead were several giant hotel chandeliers. I was surrounded by a sea of shiny black heads all singing, clapping, and joyously chanting their hymns to the Lord. Why weren't they all Jews, singing Jewish songs?

Baba sat there on a red throne, his hand keeping a rhythmic beat to the sound. In my agony, with all the heat, I looked at him and smiled. He was only 59, one year older than I was and he had some twenty million followers. If he wasn't God, he certainly was doing well!

Later that night I met Jon Gilbert. I had first heard about him in Murphet's book. Jon's story was particularly moving and meaningful to me. Most of Murphet's reports of Baba's miracles related to Indians. Here was Jon, an angry Jewish boy from New York (like me), who had been miraculously cured by Baba. Jon told us that he had gotten sick again and had returned to the ashram. Baba was helping him, but he was also taking some medication. He said he had volunteered for work in the kitchen pulling bean sprouts. He would say "Sairam" each time he pulled a sprout. Baba says that repeating the name of the Lord is a short cut to divinity.

I was shocked to find Jon looking so pale and deathly thin, saddened to find him back here and sick again, confused because it seemed that Baba had failed him.

When I told him about my mandir experience, he was sympathetic. He smiled gently and asked me if I had met Drucker. "Look for Drucker; you're going to like him."

He was right. Drucker is a God intoxicated man; his love for the Lord is infectious. Drucker said, "Don't waste your time here trying to figure out if Baba is divine; look for the divinity in yourself. First you must have faith in God and then you may have an experience. Many people come here and feel nothing at darshan and go home with nothing. They are looking for the experience first, then they will believe. You must have faith first. Jump in with both feet."

Drucker was a turning point for me. The magic of the place started to take hold. I would sit smoking outside the main gate watching the beautiful beggar children play, the roosters on top of the laundry shed, the funky cafes, the goats, cows, bullocks, donkeys, and hairless dogs wandering the street. The little souvenir store shacks lit at night by a bare bulb, all blaring out Indian bhajan-like music. Surely this must have been the way it was two thousand years ago.

Finally Baba came by at darshan and not only looked at me, but in a stern voice asked, "Where are you from?" I was so shocked I blurted out "New York," instead of Virginia. He just nodded and stopped again nearby asking another man the same question. The man said, "El Salvador," and Baba beckoned him to go for an interview. I thought, "Well, he probably needs it more than I do."

Another time Baba stopped in front of me and I gently reached out and touched his foot. It just felt smooth and warm, but no great rushes of feeling or revelation came. He even took one of my letters, but the only miracle I saw was his constant manifesting of vibhuti. I saw many people who had rings and pendants that Baba had made; they all had wonderful stories.

One personal leela from Baba was my discovery that during bhajans I could close my eyes and suddenly the whole scene I had been watching turned into beautiful shades of intense rose, pink, mauve and orange. At first I thought it was an after-image, but the scene kept changing. The audience would fade and I'd see huge palaces with gigantic walls and turrets. When Baba came outside, I could close my eyes and the whole scene would turn into a soft and yet vivid pink. He lit the sky with his presence.

I also started to see an eye. It would suddenly appear in front of my closed vision, sort of between my real eyes. I found that I could bring it in so close I could see the capillaries. I would stare at the pupil, looking for a message from the Lord. Is God watching me? The eye looked very familiar, the shape, the lines . . . yes, it was my very own. It was comforting. I had a new friend and focus for meditation.

One day at darshan I saw Drucker in the distance tending to a sick man on a stretcher. I strained but couldn't see who he was. Nervously I looked around for Jon Gilbert, but he wasn't in sight. Baba came by, stopped, chatted with Drucker, and then moved on. A group of men I recognized then came up to Drucker and together they carried the man out. Later I learned that Jon had died. I was told that he had a beautiful death; all of his friends gathered round his bed chanting "Sai Ram." Jon died with a gentle smile on his face.

Tears welled up in my eyes; I cried uncontrollably. How could Baba let him die? How could death be beautiful? Judy said later, "You don't know about Jon. You don't understand what happened in his life or about his past lives."

I sobbed, "No I don't, but I do know Jon wanted to live; that's why he was here; that's why he said one thousand Sairams a day every time he picked a bean sprout. Certainly he had karma; he was in a lot of pain, but he wanted to stay alive and pay his dues. If Baba is God, why didn't he let him live? I am tired of all these Indian miracles. I'm not going to read the books anymore. I'm fed up."

There was a funeral service. The people who knew Jon met at the Ganesha Gate. Drucker led the procession out of town, men and women walked separately, all carrying incense. Drucker and the bookstore man, Burt, chanted the vedas. I liked their deep awesome sound; it reminded me of Jews dovening.

We walked to the grave site, a deep hole in the sandy dry riverbed. I was startled to see that I knew most of the people who were there. I stood next to Massimo. He once gave a stranger his place in the first row at darshan. There was Robin, a man I used to watch play with his beautiful young blond son. So many faces that I had met or watched during these past weeks. . . all people I had written about in my journal.

The heat was unbearable. Drucker put on a gold and white yarmulke. He said we were there, not to mourn Jon, but to celebrate the Lord. He told how Jon had come as an angry young man in 1973, a terminal case with Hodgkin's Disease, how Baba had cared for him and given him eleven more years to develop spiritually. We said kaddish and sang Jewish songs; and Drucker passed around Jon's vibhuti box which was filled with Jon's ashes. One by one we sprinkled them into the gaping hole in the ground.

That night, in the middle of the night, I woke up suddenly. I could see Drucker with that gold yarmulke on his head. I asked myself, "How often does a man die here? How often does a man die here and have a Jewish funeral? How often does Drucker, a man I know, conduct the ceremony? How often does a man die here that I know!" At that moment all of the faces of all the people from the funeral suddenly came to life like characters in a movie. I sobbed with joy. This was Baba's divinity play. Baba knows me. He cares. He orchestrated the whole scenario for my learning, for my benefit, so that I could understand and lose my fear of death.

I felt, at last, I had made a dent in my protective armor. There were even moments when I thought Baba was God; but in the next instant I would ask myself, "How could God's eyes be bloodshot? He coughs, he sweats . . ."

Kasturi says that Baba likes to churn us up. Baba likes butter. The only way you get butter from milk is to churn.

As we left Puttaparthi, I was feeling very clean after being without marijuana and alcohol for almost a month. No promises; I didn't even tell Judy; I thought I would just see how it felt to go without them for a while. We stopped off in Hawaii and stayed at a beautiful beach resort where I would normally start drinking before noon. I used to have at least two or three very large drinks before dinner, then a half bottle of wine with my meal followed by white brandy. In between I'd be smoking a joint, just to feel a little more out of it . . . I liked the feeling of drifting off into a deep sleep. Strange, considering all my fears about my life being snuffed out.

I stopped completely, cold turkey; it was effortless. At first I didn't feel very different. I was just pleased with how easy it was.

Judy was overjoyed. She had never told me, but before going to see Baba, she had prayed to him saying, "Baba, if you are all these books say you are, I only want one thing—to have Jack stop drinking alcohol and smoking marijuana."

I began to notice a few subtle changes, like deciding not to lie anymore; or I'd find my feelings just welling up inside me, find myself crying while telling stories about some of my Baba experiences.

It was very gradual. I read many more Baba books, started listening to bhajan tapes; and I actually began watching my words, thoughts and actions. When I felt impatient, I would remember waiting on a line at the ashram and start repeating, "Sairam, Sairam" over and over again. I'd forget to say thanks for my food, so much so that I had to promise myself that if I forgot again, I would have to get down on my knees to give thanks.

I was, and still am, of two minds: mine, and the monkey's. Sometimes I talk about Baba as if he were God. I tell my children that God has incarnated as a human to light the lamp of love and bring back a rebirth of spirituality.

My son Adam brings me up short by saying, "Well Dad, you always have been into power!" My children are young adults. They are pleased that I no longer smoke grass and drink, but they find all my talk about God too much.

Adam says, "Why does he need a bodyguard, you know, the big guy who keeps the people back? If he's God, why can't he hold them in line with his mind? Why doesn't he get on television, appearing on every channel at the same time? Then everyone will know he's God!" I tell them it is not possible to prove that Baba is divine, that you just have to accept it; but sometimes I wish it were possible.

Other times my kids ask, "If Baba is God, then why doesn't he do something about all the wars, famine, injustice, and suffering?"

I try to tell them that Baba is here to raise man's spiritual consciousness, that then, and only then, can there be peace and harmony. Baba says that if he were to simply wave his hand and make everything perfect, we would soon return to the same conditions we have now. He says it is up to us to find our own spiritual rebirth. Sometimes I wonder why Baba can't or won't include the perfection of human consciousness in this wave of his hand. Perhaps if he did, there wouldn't be any reason for us to incarnate.

I want to live by Baba's five principles of truth, right conduct, love, peace and nonviolence. I have started to pray and say the gayatri mantra each morning and before sleep. When thinking bad thoughts, I catch myself, and say "Sairam." I used to love to gossip, but now I stop myself, at least most of the time.

I truly believe that our ego and attachments are the root cause of pain and suffering. Without attachments we can loosen desire; without desire we can be free of anger, hate, jealousy, greed, envy and pride. Without our egos, we can be humble, and hopefully seek and find God. Baba says that he knows our past, present, and future. Then how can there be free will? Where is the basis for praise or blame? I liked my old rules. It took me a long time to feel good about myself. Now that I have finally gotten a sense of pride from worldly success, it seems it wasn't "me" or "mine" at all—but it was God's grace.

I've read that the only choice we have is to turn towards God or away from him. It's really not a bad tradeoff because if I place myself in God's hands, then I am protected; I don't have to spin the dice anymore. I am his! But if everything has been decided, then why try and do anything? The answer seems to be that being human, or in a physical body, means that most of us will not always turn towards God, so we need to live our lives as if we had free will.

Baba says, "*Life is a challenge, meet it. Life is a game, play it. Life is love, enjoy it. Life is a dream, realize it.*"

Baba tells a story about a dog entering a room where all of the walls are mirrored. The dog seeing many dogs, barks. When a man enters the same room, he sees his many reflections. He takes pleasure in discovering the different aspects of himself. Baba explains that in the world we see billions of people and objects appearing to be different. He says that these differences are like the reflections in the mirror; they are illusory. Baba says there is great joy in getting acquainted with, and learning to love, the many aspects of ourselves in the people and objects around us. He says he is in our hearts; I hope to find him.

Baba says, look at the ocean. See the waves swelling, rolling, breaking into foaming surf. You see different forms: water, waves, foam, and bubbles, yet you do not question for an instant that all you see is one ocean. You can understand because of the brief span of time it takes for the different forms to merge and blend as one. If only we can make a leap of faith, we will know that everything is his creation and that we are part of him. To see ourselves as separate is to miss the joy of knowing that we are him, that we are all divine; surely then, we can see and love ourselves in every person, blade of grass, and star in the universe.

My values continue to change. In all my life I have never done any service work. I have never intentionally hurt anyone, but doing good for others was an activity I either ignored or hoped others would handle. At Baba's 60th birthday, I was asked by Hal Honig, a Regional Director, if I would try and set up a Baba Study Group in Virginia. I hesitated. I didn't want to say yes and then not do it. You can get in big trouble lying to God! The more I thought about it the better I liked it. Here was a built-in opportunity to test myself, to find out if I could make it on this spiritual path. I welcomed the idea of meeting and being around Baba people.

I always liked the quote: "*Hands that serve are holier than lips that pray.*" Now I would have my chance; only this time I vowed not to run this group like one of my former corporations. I hoped to do the work with love and trust that Baba will do the rest.

I no longer feel I have to make it happen. Our study group started out with twelve, and now we are down to seven regulars. Our first service project was to build a vegetable garden at "Liberty House," a local nursing home for the aged. I was a bit nervous seeing the majority of the 109 patients in wheelchairs. As a child I had to push my mother everywhere, and I guess I didn't get enough, or at least I didn't do it with love, so now Baba is giving me another chance. On our very first day I sat with an old patient who just liked to sing hymns. We sang "On-ward Christian Soldiers." I remembered it from the time my step-father made me go to the Christian Science church.

Soon another old man, looking depressed, joined us. I asked him how he felt and he said, "Not good, a man just died." I nodded trying to offer some comfort, but I wondered, how come the first thing out of this man's mouth dealt with my own fear of dying? In the next second the man started to tell me how afraid he was of losing his money. Again, the man had tapped directly into my own major concern with money. At that mo-ment I smiled, realizing this was surely Baba's way of saying hello and indicating he was indeed watching.

Another of Baba's teachings, putting a ceiling on my material desires, is slowly becoming a part of my life. I still buy too many things, but more and more I ask before making a pur-chase: do I really want it, does it serve a meaningful purpose, does it hurt or deprive anyone? I truly want to give up being attached to things. My goal is to treat objects as if they were rented furniture in a beautiful hotel room—enjoy, and yet walk away without regrets at check-out time.

When I was a child, I think I gave up God because there didn't seem to be any way for him to see and know everything and be everywhere. Now I'm told that Baba is omniscient, om-nipresent, and omnipotent. He knows everything; he is everywhere, and he is all powerful. Why not? Certainly the Lord is more than a giant universal computer. It seems I've come full circle, and it's with a great sense of relief that I can begin now to "Let go and Let God." I'm ready to be captured, ready to stop talking and just do the work I should be doing.

In Vedanta and Sai literature there are many references to bliss and the joy of becoming one with the Lord. The only liberation I want is complete freedom from my old fears of death. Merging is like a raindrop falling into the ocean—it's gone; it's not a drop anymore. I'm not yet ready to give up my still precious sense of self awareness. I don't want to be the sugar; I want to taste it.

Baba says, "*Enjoy*," and "*End Joy.*"

Slowly now, when I think about dying, I imagine peacefully letting go and leaving my body. I keep hearing him say, "*You are not the body; shed it like a worn out overcoat.*" And I'll think, "That's what I want to do, go out smiling with Sai Ram on my lips." But suddenly my old fears leap out: "Suppose it's all a hoax—that you just die, squished out like a fly, zapped into oblivion?"

Then I laugh, "Even so, there isn't a better way to live than following Baba's teachings."

I believe I know now what I want to become. **One . . .**

> *Who has no hatred towards any being,*
> *is friendly, kind and compassionate;*
> *Who does not feel that anything belongs to him,*
> *And bears sorrow and joy with equanimity.* [2]

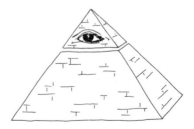

---

[2] The words of Sri Krishna in the *Bhagavad Gita.*

You may wonder: "Why would God pay any attention to me? What could I possibly offer to Him that He would accept when the entire cosmos is already His? If even angels and gods cannot see Him, what chance is there for me?" But such self-demeaning and belittling thoughts will get you nowhere. As long as you think this way, you will be unable to earn the grace of God and be fit to serve Him. Give no place to such displays of weakness. You must install God in your heart and say to Him, "Beloved Lord! I know You occupy the entire universe, but You are also here in my heart. With all my power I will keep You here, firmly established within me. You are, it is true, the greatest of the great; but You are also the smallest of the small. In that minute aspect You reside always in my heart." If you have this firm faith in yourself and a steadfast resolve to fix God unalterably in your heart, you will surely attain Him.

—Sathya Sai Baba

AN EXTRAORDINARY JOURNEY

Barbara Bozzani

To know where we are going in this journey through life, it is sometimes helpful to know where we have been. We are all God's children, but he has placed each of us in a unique set of circumstances. The influences of family, friends and environment all leave marks, sometimes scars, on the psyche. I had the good fortune to be born into a family that valued high morals and sound ethics. Truthfulness was a code learned early in life. But the other side of my early training was lacking in some areas. My family never spoke of God or love nor was there much joy or creative expression. These came later when I discovered the world beyond my home environment.

My mother conveyed the impression that an open display of affection or the giving of praise and reassurance to children would spoil them. After all, it's a tough world and we must be able to deal with harsh realities. Perhaps it was the deep hurt she felt from her own difficult upbringing, coupled with the pain of separation from my father when I was still very young. After the separation, as an only child, I was the focal point of her attention, and I felt her deep concern for my well-being and security. She did an admirable job in a time when women, as single parents, were often shunned by society. She taught me to be neat and clean, to hold my head high and to tell the truth.

Hard work was another of her teachings for which I am grateful. Because of her German Lutheran ethic, I worked part-time from the age of 11. It was sometimes quite difficult to balance a baby-sitting or a mother's helper job with my studies and school activities. Later I took on the task of making all my own clothes, and was rather good at it.

My mother's sense of responsibility should have been somewhat relieved when she met and married a fine Greek gentleman, but the habit of worry was deeply ingrained in her personality.

My stepfather, besides easing our financial difficulties, opened the way for some cultural expression. We traveled a little, read books together, went to museums and talked of worldly events. Still there was no spiritual interest shown by either parent. But I began to make my own religious investigations.

I had gone to various Sunday schools and churches with friends, and had always felt great joy when hymns were sung and Bible stories were told. But, much to my dismay, I found that many of the "church people" who attentively listened to Christian teachings, such as "Love thy neighbor as thyself," were practicing some form of prejudice in their daily lives.

When I was still quite young, a relative whom I trusted made an uncomplimentary comment about a group of Catholic nuns. I was shocked and hurt by this person's criticism of the good nuns who gave so much service to the world. Becoming aware of hypocrisy in those I loved was both confusing and disheartening.

As I grew older and became aware of the terrible things that happen in the world, I began to think that a good and loving God would never let crimes and atrocities happen to innocent people. My simplistic conclusion, as a disenchanted teenager, was that there must not be a God, and that religious beliefs must be a form of escapism for those who could not face reality.

The years rolled by, and near the completion of my education, I met a charming young man. On July 4, 1952, we were married in the midst of much celebrating of the national holiday. Bob was then an officer in the United States Navy. Our married life centered around parties and social gatherings, and all in all was most agreeable for both of us, yet there was something lacking, like one small missing piece of a puzzle.

With each new event I thought, this is the thing that will make life complete. Upon Bob's discharge from the Navy, he went into his family's automobile business. By then we had one beautiful daughter, and two years later another baby girl, both of whom brought us great joy. Before the arrival of our son, we moved to a larger home. Bob now had his own prosperous business and our family was complete. Who could expect more? But we both felt an inner restlessness.

At that time I had a friend who always seemed to be calm and peaceful. When I asked her to divulge her secret formula for composure, she said that she practiced hatha yoga and that she would be happy to take me to meet her teacher. I took to hatha yoga with great interest and in a few years began teaching classes.

During this period I also attended classes given by Indra Devi, who instructed us in the ancient, classic postures and later astounded us with stories of her spiritual preceptor, Sri Sathya Sai Baba. Her stories created a longing within me to go to exotic India and see this reputedly amazing being. The longing became an obsession. In the later part of 1973, I convinced my husband that we should travel with a group of Westerners to see Baba at his ashram near the small village of Puttaparthi in South India. Sai Baba had reportedly performed wonders such as Christ had done. My curiosity could not be assuaged; I had to see for myself.

My husband was going through a rather difficult period in his life and was less than enthusiastic about taking a trip to India. Nevertheless, in February of 1974, off we went, with about twenty other curious pilgrims, for an unforgettable journey.

On the first day in the ashram one of our travel companions came by the room and told us to get ready for darshan (being in the presence of a great spiritual being). Not knowing at the time what darshan was or how to get ready for it, we had to be advised: first bathe, then dress in clean clothing, and finally, proceed to the temple area to quietly await the appearance of Sri Sathya Sai Baba. All this I did while still being the ultimate tourist, not taking any of it too seriously. Instead, I was thinking what a good story all this would be to share with friends and yoga students at home.

Much to my surprise, when Sai Baba did appear and walk before the crowd, I felt riveted to the spot and could not take my eyes from him. I had seen many pictures of Sai Baba, but was not prepared for such a deeply moving experience. His natural grace and charm were beguiling. I forgot all the discomforts of jet lag and sitting in the hot sun wrapped in a sari. Something about his demeanor made my cold heart begin to soften; I felt a surge of joy. For a long time thereafter, that joy felt like gentle ocean waves sweeping over me, then receding. I wanted to stay enveloped in that oceanic feeling, but it was too elusive. I didn't know then how fortunate we were, for Baba had told one of our group that he would see us the next day.

We all arrived promptly on the temple veranda at the designated hour and were ushered into a large room. There were no embellishments, just a simple wooden chair on a platform for Baba. The rest of us tried to be comfortable on the cement floor, and then it happened again! As Sai Baba entered the room, all thoughts of discomfort disappeared, and the waves of joy took over. How could his presence cause such a reaction? He never sat in the special chair, but seemed to prefer relaxing on the edge of the platform, standing before us or moving through the group.

Baba gave us a mini-discourse; and to this day I don't remember a word he said, only the soft melodic tones of his voice and a feeling of happiness. At some point in the talk he manifested a ring for a woman in our group. I was pleased because one of my secret wishes had been to see some miracles. Indeed, I saw it clearly, as it appeared right under my nose. I was collecting experiences, and that was a pretty good one. But what next?

Some days later as we were sitting on the veranda waiting to be called into Baba's interview room, a handsome but distressed Indian family were ushered into the small inner room. The father was carrying his son, who was about 9 years old; the boy was wearing white socks which didn't really conceal his badly deformed feet. His spindly legs indicated that he had never run or played like other children. I felt a tug at my heart. I was grateful for the three healthy children we had left in the care of their grandparents in California.

After some time, the door swung open; and, wonder of wonders, the family emerged, all of them weeping tears of joy. The young boy was walking on wobbly legs like a newborn fawn, his large brown eyes sparkling. I didn't even try to control my own tears.

Baba came out and gave some final instructions to the parents; then he turned to me and asked, "Why are you crying? Don't cry; it's the first time he has walked." I replied through tears, "That's why I'm crying." He then gave me a look I have come to know so well—the most kind and compassionate smile I had ever seen—and he said in the softest of tones, "I know, I know."

I wanted that moment to last forever, but in an instant he had changed his demeanor and was showing deep concern for another of his children.

Soon it was our turn to be alone with Baba. Our first private interview was an overwhelming experience. Bob and I and Sai Baba stood close together as Baba asked questions. He addressed me first, asking simple questions like, "How many children do you have?" At that moment I was at a loss for words. He smiled indulgently and answered the question himself, saying, "Three." In the meantime I stood mute—unable to communicate. I must have appeared more than foolish, but Baba was kind as he understands all human conditions and frailties. During those few minutes he outlined the character—both the strengths and weaknesses—of each of our children. The passing years have revealed him to be one hundred percent accurate.

His attention then turned to Bob, and they spoke of business matters while Sai manifested some vibhuti (holy ash) and stroked Bob's chest and heart area with the ash saying, "He is a good man, a good man." This clear sign of loving approval caused Bob to do something I had never seen him do before—he burst into tears and cried like a helpless child. Sai Baba said,

"Business gives you no satisfaction, but all that will change."
Bob brightened at that reassurance.

Swami, as he often refers to himself, turned again to me
and said, "Be patient. You need to learn to be patient." The
interview was over, and I was still mute as we left. It took a
long time to come back to earth. It had been the most unusual
experience of my life, but I still failed to see that Sri Sathya Sai
Baba was a divine being. I could only perceive that he was special
and that he invoked higher ideals and emotions in me than I
had ever known before.

While on the airplane back to the United States, we started
planning our next trip to India. Already, we were being drawn
back as if by some magnetic force. Bob, in a lighthearted spirit,
began to tease me about Swami's comments on my being impatient. I immediately became defensive, annoyed and obviously
impatient. Later we both had a good laugh at my narrow viewpoint and inability to accept criticism, even though it had been
given so gently by Baba. I promised myself, then and there, to
work on the problem of impatience.

Upon returning home, we resumed our activities, but somehow our lives had changed. Bob and I still cared about our old
friends but found it difficult—even impossible—to resume the
old round of social events. Bob dove deeply into reading everything about Sathya Sai Baba. I, on the other hand, had pressured
him to go with me to India but was left feeling incomplete and
confused by the experience.

In 1975 we returned to India, first touring and then continuing on to attend a World Conference of Sri Sathya Sai Or-
ganizations and Baba's 50th birthday. There had been only one
prior experience in my background to prepare me for life in an
ashram, and this time it was more difficult because of the large
crowds that had gathered for the conference and birthday
celebrations.

Again we received interviews, and Bob was given a lovely
ring with Baba's likeness. In fact, many people were given "calling

cards," as Swami calls the small gifts like rings and lockets, which he manifests.

Seeing the faces of those who received these items from Baba's own hand generated a feeling of great joy, and I began to long for one of those talismans. In fact, I became obsessed. But the more I wished for something, the more frequent were Baba's gifts to others! In one interview he actually gave divine tokens to ladies in front, in back and on either side of me! I must have looked green with envy, but all I got from Baba was a mischievous smile.

He often says, "I give you what you want, so that you will want what I have come to give." But what did that message have to do with my desire to have one of his small gifts? What was to be learned from this spiritual stuff anyway? Why did intense feelings seem to be tearing me apart?

The following year back home, I suffered from doubts and periods of loneliness and depression. Confusion mounted, and I wondered if I truly wanted to give up the old social round, the conspicuous consumption and self-indulgence. But those shallow activities no longer offered pleasure, nor did anything else. I was on an emotional roller coaster. Baba has said, "Sometimes I must break the heart in order to enter it." Perhaps that was what was happening.

Meanwhile my husband was drawing closer to Sai Baba. He insisted that we have devotional songs (bhajans) sung in our home and that we study Swami's teachings. In spite of mixed emotions at this time, I was looking forward to our next trip to India, for those journeys had become annual events of pain and pleasure. The attraction to Sai Baba was still impossible to explain.

The next year we took our three children and Bob's mother to India. Baba showered grace upon all of them. I felt completely out of step; I contracted the flu and remained ill during the whole journey. At one point in Bombay, I expressed my wish to allocate some worldly possessions to our children, for I felt certain I would die before returning home. I must have been having hallucinations from the fever, or wallowing in self-pity. Probably both. It was quite impossible to eat, and I became more and more weak. I scribbled a letter to Baba on hotel stationery asking for his help.

Bob hand-carried that letter to the Dharmakshetra, Baba's place of residence in Bombay, where Swami was scheduled to give a discourse. Baba walked past my husband and accepted my desperate note. All during his discourse he held that letter, making graceful hand gestures and pointing the envelope toward the thousands who had assembled to hear him. All this was not known to me until later, but I do remember feeling better during that time.

The next day I had recovered enough to go with my family to the Dharmakshetra where Baba received us. He held my hand during most of the interview and seemed concerned about my health, telling me: "Eat." The next day, aboard our plane for the long flight back to the United States, my appetite was insatiable. But even more important, my heart had opened a little wider and my doubts were drifting away; perhaps this was my spiritual renaissance.

During our first trip to India I had observed an unusual custom: many devotees wanting to touch or even kiss Baba's feet. My first reaction to this was negative. On the following trip, I thought it was fine for Indians to practice this custom but not a western lady. During the third trip, however, I had a great longing to touch those perfectly formed, fragrant feet, and I asked Baba several times for padnamaskar, as it is called; I was told: "Wait, wait." In the meantime, the longing grew. Only at the last moment of our last day in India did Baba allow me the privilege. He stepped forward, pointed to his feet and said, "Do." I fell to my knees, knowing in the depths of my heart that this was the most profound and sacred opportunity of my lifetime, a moment of great magnitude, the beginning of surrender.

In the following years, Bob and I journeyed to India to be near our beloved teacher once or twice annually. Occasionally one or all of the children accompanied us. Baba always seemed to bestow his special grace on the young and they responded favorably.

At this point it has been nearly sixteen years since I first heard of Sri Sathya Sai Baba, and I am actually horrified to think what life would be like without him. At best it would be an endless stream of empty events and meaningless activities. Certainly my life was headed in that direction before I knew Swami.

Baba exhorts his followers to serve. He says, "Service to humanity is service to God." My service has taken the form of editing and publishing the *Sathya Sai Newsletter*. Highly qualified devotees donate many hours to create a quarterly publication devoted to the phenomenon of Bhagavan Sri Sathya Sai Baba and his teachings. Working on the national "Newsletter" is a joy as well as an awesome responsibility because I am now convinced that Baba is the Lord incarnate; a complete avatar with all the powers, glory and divine love that this engenders. He is the embodiment of love, and has come to re-establish righteousness in the world. Only God can do that.

Baba is our greatest teacher, for there are lessons in what he does as well as what he does not do. For example, I used to ponder: why, if he is God, does he allow starvation and devastating disease to occur? Baba has said that he could change all that in an instant, but in a short time the same human tragedies would return and the world would be as badly off as before. Is it possible, then, that we do these things to ourselves? Baba confirms what the Catholic Church has said for many years: there is an abundance of food in the world but that the distribution is not equitable. Surely we can't blame God for this lack of concern for our fellow human beings. We can and do blame governments for not coming to the aid of less fortunate nations. However, Baba would have us look within our own hearts and ask what we as individuals can do to help our less fortunate brothers and sisters.

In regard to disease, I used to wonder why Baba does not cure at least those who come to him seeking his help. Now I understand that he seldom interferes with the individual's need to undergo certain negative experiences. Even though such experiences may seem tragic to us, in another perception, they could be considered grace, or the paying of karmic debts. Sooner or later we must all pay our debts. Since God knows our past, present and future, why not surrender everything to him? Then body, mind and soul are in his keeping forever more.

The lessons have been numerous, but my own experience has confirmed that concepts must be put into practice. I was struck, for example, by the realization that I must forgive and even learn to love, the father who abandoned me so long ago. Swami declares that it is most important to love our parents, for they have given us human birth. He continues by saying, "It is only through a human birth that we can realize God." And, further, there are souls in heaven waiting for the good fortune to be born.

In years past I had been critical of some people for their subtle prejudice. Baba tells us that we have no right to judge others; often they are reflecting our own inner thoughts and feelings. Perhaps truly learning tolerance consists of not being intolerant of the intolerance of others.

In a recent interview when asked to define ego, Baba quickly responded, "It is ignorance, ignorance."

According to Baba marriage provides an opportunity to eliminate "this greatest human stumbling block."

I can vouch for this as I recall the many situations where Baba has had us face the realities of married life. For example, on one of our trips Bob and I arrived at Prasanthi Nilayam in the midst of a heated disagreement. Later Swami scolded both of us for arguing. On another occasion I was rather annoyed with Bob but kept it to myself. Swami approached me during darshan and said, "Always fighting with husband."

I responded, "No Swami, not fighting." He then said, "Yes—arguing here," pointing to his head.

He has told us, "Marriage is like sandpaper rubbing away each other's egotism." And his teaching concerning the correct attitude in the relationship is quite specific: The wife serves the husband, and the husband has the task of protecting and caring for the wife. Each loves God, that spark of divinity inherent in the other.

Indeed, I have learned more about the roles of husband and wife from our beloved Baba than one could learn from any marriage manual.

I have already mentioned my desire for a token of Swami's divinity, one of his small gifts "manufactured" from thin air. After several trips to India and many interviews, it finally happened! At the time, I concluded that my motives were totally incorrect—after all, I had seen, talked with, and been given sound advice by, the Lord himself. Who could ask for more?

The very next interview Baba asked me, "What do you want?" I said, "You, Swami, you." He smiled indulgently, like a parent who is about to reward a small child with an ice cream cone. With a wave of that beautiful hand, he presented to me a ring with the likeness of Shirdi Sai Baba (his previous incarnation) in bas-relief. I was thrilled; it was a magic moment of sheer delight.

He placed the ring on my right index finger, which I've come to feel is very significant. I must confess to being afraid at times, to say "no" because someone might not approve of me. I truly think the likeness of Shirdi Sai Baba has given courage to my convictions. Placing the ring on the right index finger was, I feel, meant to make me more assertive, for it is this finger we use to indicate or emphasize a point. Swami has never confirmed this. It is my own perception; I only know that something has helped.

These are but a few of the lessons and experiences I've had since consciously coming into Sai Baba's orbit. I say "consciously" because I now feel that he has always been guiding and protecting me. His love is so great that he even watches over those who do not accept his divinity.

My husband and I often have sensed his presence in both home and office, by the tell-tale fragrance of jasmine or vibhuti. We will be busily concentrating on a task when, suddenly, his fragrance will occur, giving rise to an inexpressible feeling of peace and joy.

Indeed he is with each of us always and in all ways. To know him, all we need do is love God and seek his love in return. What better way to spend the rest of this extraordinary journey?

I do not encourage adoration of just one name and one form, particularly my present name and present form. I have no wish to draw people toward Me, away from the worship of my other names and forms. You may infer from what you call my miracles that I am attracting people and causing attachments to Me and Me alone. But that is not so. These so-called miracles are merely spontaneous proofs of Divine Majesty. There is no need to change your chosen God to adopt a new one when you have seen me or heard me. Continue your worship of your chosen God along the lines already familiar to you and you will find you are coming nearer and nearer to me, for all names are mine and all forms are mine.

—Sathya Sai Baba

SEEKING LOVE

Bea Flaig

Where shall my story start when I wish to tell of my love for Sathya Sai Baba and how he has changed my life? Since our lives are so woven into time and space, so much a part of our experiences, of people we know and of those whom we do not realize we know—since there is so much more to our God story—let me write that which my heart is telling.

I know that through my youth, I searched for that source from which I would do good and see good. I believed it to be my mind, for never would I call it God, whose image was that of a bearded old man in a heavenly sky.

I later discovered that many were searching just as I was, but they pictured a form, a God that could and would do all for them. My belief was that man had to do for himself, and my search was in how, on Earth, I could improve. In time this ego was to be transformed.

Gradually, through my first teacher, Hilda Charlton, did I begin to understand the meaning of God and spirituality. It was through Hilda that I was led to God incarnate, Sathya Sai. My heart was captured slowly, for mine is such that works slowly, but surely. Once having grasped the love, it hangs on tenaciously in the face of all adversity, for its foundation is strong.

In 1974, when I first set out upon this path of glory, I wrote the following poem:

A child—middle aged
Looks for a love,
 Not physical.

An adult—child-like
Seeking her light,
 Holy, spiritual.

I remember wondering why I wrote it—what did it really mean? It was a week later that my confusion took the form of a lament:

Love, breathe it in
Love, breathe it out
          I can't
Poor Bea, wants to believe
          But can't!

and ended with:

Love, breathe it in
Love, breathe it out
          I can't!
Poor girl, yearns to have faith
          But can't

I did try to believe, but I had so much difficulty. Those of us who have lived for many years without an awareness of God in our hearts, who have led a life devoid of belief in miracles or the power of prayer and healing, may only be awakened by LOVE, pure, unconditional love—and some part of me knew this even as I lamented.

As I progressed along the path, meditating many hours, determined to solve the questions, "Who is God?" "What is God?" my narrow mind began to be aware of a new world. I saw people getting healed; I heard stories that boggled my mind; I saw vibhuti manifest on pictures and statues in my house.

But the mind is a demon! No matter what wondrous events I witnessed or heard of, there was the doubting mind, ever present, conjuring up worldly reasons for everything.

"Everything is within you," Baba says. I did not understand this truth; I had no atma, soul consciousness; it was all my mind, my intellect that was the creator. (I laugh as I write this, for indeed the mind does create—it is the creator of this *maya* in which we live, the illusion that takes us in cycles from the heights of joy to the depths of despair.)

But God is ever patient, ever gracious. Hilda continued to share her love with me along with her stories of an 18 year stay in India. She told me of the wonders of Sai Baba. They sounded fantasic, but I just could not believe them. And then, Swami's face began to appear more and more in my meditations. "Imagination, mind pictures," I thought to myself. But my heart was, at last, beginning to stir.

I have a small theory about our path to God. When things are rough and we're not advancing the way we want to, when we are almost about to give up; something happens to blow our mind, something which gives us a taste of GOD, and we're hooked! We know that we must go on, never giving up the search for another God vision, another experience of euphoria in the sea of bliss.

I tell the following story because it has kept me on the path all these years despite the many hours of despair. It turned the key to another plane of consciousness, and its recollection continues to remind me of what true love is. In truth, what else is worthy of our aspirations?

It was in 1975. I was spending hours meditating—before work, during work, after work, in the middle of the night. It seemed beyond my control. I would end each meditation with, "God, reveal yourself to me." Nothing seemed to satisfy me, not the touch of peace, nor the spurts of love, nor the images that came, for doubt was always rearing its disconcerting self. I felt unfulfilled.

I remember that night so well. My husband brought home a statue of Ganesha. The moment he showed it to me, I could feel an attraction. It was something I could not understand, but I felt a warmth creep into me. I felt a sense of energy hit me

between the eyes as I touched it. After dinner when I went into
the bedroom where we had left the statue, I noticed that vibhuti
had formed.

"Meditate, meditate," my body cried. I picked up the statue,
went into the puja room and sat down in front of the altar.
With Ganesha still in my hand, I repeated my mantra and moved
the beads of my rosary. I was filled with such a strong desire to
know what the sages were telling, to experience the glory of
which the saints spoke. I could feel every part of me crying out
to understand, to be a child of God. I called every name I
could think of—every saint, every holy name, but never did
I call on Sai Baba. I cannot tell you why, but I did not call
his name.

And as I called and pleaded, I became plagued with doubts.
Evil thoughts began to attack me—pricks in my mind and body.
"Fool, there is no God . . . You can't trust them . . . Don't you
know it's all a lie . . ." On and on it went, nasty ideas about
God, about my path, about people I believed in, all coming at
me. I knew not what it was all about, or how it came on. I was
an onlooker, observing a terrifying scene. I could sense fear grow-
ing, and then I saw myself stiffen and with great determination
I heard myself say, "Get away. I don't want to hear you. Go
away, I don't believe you. You don't know what you are talking
about. I want GOD!" I remember that part. I remember the
determination. I also know that something happened, that there
was an unaccountable space of time and the next thing I could
recall was an opening above me and I was propelled into a sea
of expanse, a universe of stars, expanding, expanding . . . and
ecstasy started pouring through me, washing me, loving me—
and I heard a voice, somewhere far off in the distance, a voice
that I recognized as being me but not me. I could hear it saying,
"I GIVE MYSELF TO THEE, SAI BABA."

Sai Baba! Sai Baba, a name I hadn't even called! Sai Baba,
God who had reached my soul!

That night I slept and dreamed. I dreamed that I was being buried in a grave, and all around me people were dancing merrily. I felt no fear or remorse. When I awoke the next morning, the dream was still vividly with me. I felt that it was connected to my meditation experience, that it marked the death of my old self and a rebirth. That summer I made plans for my first visit to India, to see Swami in his physical form.

I wish I could say that I had been truly reborn, and that my thoughts, words and deeds were always pure. No. Although I had been blessed by God, I had still to earn that kingdom, if it were to be mine forever!

My first visit to Swami was amazing on all accounts. I will not delve into all the stories at this time, but by now you know all the layers which he had to uncover. There was an instant interview that resulted in great awe and pain. After that, in between a period of being totally ignored, there was the thrill of being in his presence at a wedding, and, finally, the bliss of another interview before leaving for home.

Still, much remained unanswered. I was so involved with my own advancement toward God, that I did not see God in front of me, nor could I see my own God-self. Oh, I did see Baba's poetic step, his smile that brought warmth to all, the changes that he brought about in some of the handicapped people he had taken in for interviews—but these did not linger with me.

"Swami, talk to me, teach me directly, solve all my problems," were my cries, my worldly ego overtaking the glimpse of divinity I had been given.

And so the years moved on. I returned to India, to his lotus feet, received the interviews, the blessings, the materializations, and still I cried out. God always seemed one step beyond my reach. I was not a student of Theosophy; my knowledge of the Bible and other holy books was negligible. I was not in touch with psychic phenomena, or third eye vision. However, my thoughts did start to change, for I began to say to myself, "Surely, somewhere on this path, I must be useful. In some way I might be of concrete service to the spirit of God."

The awareness of how I was to serve as his instrument also progressed slowly. At one point I read Swami's declaration, "The end of education is character." Here at last was my message! Was I not a teacher? Then why not put these ideas into the classroom? I delved deeper into the Bal Vikas program and how I might use it with my students in the public school system. The results were amazing. It could work! Where once I would go to sleep with the worry of how to face another day of class-room feuds, of children's disrespect for one another, of their lack of self-worth, and would wake up with the same fears, I now began to feel a change, a glimmer of hope, a realization that working with values would change the children. God was offering me another chance, a chance to rectify the mistakes I had made in bringing up my own children, a chance to be of use in this lifetime.

And changes did begin. The changes were not only occur-ring in the children, but I, too, was changing. I became lighter, freer, happier. That which had borne upon me so heavily began to wash away. I knew what my future would have to be. I had to explore what Swami was now calling Education in Human Values.

And so I applied for a sabbatical to write a values cur-riculum for use in my district public schools. Another great transformation was about to take place. I had always been wor-ried about money; and now I was faced with a cut in salary and with many plans for travel, yet I was not at all concerned. I'm not sure how there was enough money—but there we were that year, my husband and I, traveling to Canada, Israel, France and India. And as we traveled, I researched the many values programs that were in existence.

In the summer of 1983, I once again arrived in India, this time to participate in the International Conference on EHV. I knew my answer would be found here. Little did I know that I would find more than just my role in EHV.

Baba was as beautiful and gracious as ever. On the darshan line he would tell the New York participants, "Yes, yes. I will see you." He would often repeat this to my husband and others on the men's side. It never happened! It was the first time I had not had an interview. But I was not the same person either. I found myself listening to every word Baba was saying in his discourses in the Poornachandra. Every sound that came from him was a gem for me. He served us well, showering us with unconditional love and showing us his true form. For the first time, I came to realize that I was indeed in the presence of God. I knew what it meant.

He came to our small meetings promising, "No one shall leave without their questions answered." And so it came to be. We were permitted to submit written questions which he proceeded to answer. We were in his presence for hours. Invariably when a new problem crossed my mind, I would hear him give me the solution, even as he spoke on another topic. This went on for days, and his magnanimity overwhelmed me. I had to begin thinking seriously about how I could serve.

Baba fed our minds, our hearts, our souls and even our bodies. When we were served lunch in the canteen, it was so beautiful to watch him as he went down the aisles, asking if we had enough, if we were happy . . . ever GIVING, GIVING. "How much can one take," I thought, "without giving in return?"

This is my new birth, my new work. I have been granted faith and belief. I know what love can really be. As long as Baba lets me help in his task of Education in Human Values, I shall be there. I don't think he expects us to be specialists in teaching EHV, but rather to be specialists in life, meeting its challenges with equanimity and love.

As I conclude this story, I flash upon the day my mother died. I recall the pledge I made as a young 15-year-old confused by my loss. "When I grow up, I'm going to do something for this world. I'm going to help cure cancer."

It is now 45 years down the road, and God has granted me my wish. In my final surrender to him, I have become his instrument. The cancer that is eating away at our character, the cancer that is wiping out righteousness in this world, the cancer that is shattering our peace and causing our physical cancer—that is the cancer which Sathya Sai Baba is now transforming. Thus, shall he bring to all mankind TRUTH, RIGHT ACTION, PEACE, LOVE and NON-VIOLENCE.

Love in action is right action; as speech is truth; as thought is peace; as understanding is non-violence.

—Sathya Sai Baba

IT'S ALL GOD
Allen S. Levy

It's a snowy day in mid-November, New York City. A premature winter has blanketed the concrete metropolis in white, almost magically creating an illusionary aura of purity throughout New York, a city, not unlike most, steadily sinking into the mire of greed, lust and self-aggrandizement.

The twentieth patient of the week has just left the office. Like many, she feels lonely and lost in a world where spiritual values are often disrespected and the word of God is ignored. In despair she feels a lack of love in her life that most of us also feel, caught on a planet suffering under the torturous burden of material values and perspectives. Modern day Earth—a world where truth is denied, righteousness reviled, non-violence only an ideal, peace of mind a dream, and unconditional love merely a vision.

I feel her sadness. I feel her pain. Her loneliness becomes my loneliness, and her despair becomes my despair, but only for a short time. For I have found a way out of this darkness, this hopelessness. My isolation and imprisonment have given way to openness and freedom. And the helplessness I used to feel has now given way to helpfulness by the grace of God.

Contemplating my life and the advent of the avatar within it, my attention is drawn back, back in time through the years to when I was first born. First born spiritually, that is, into a consciousness of God.

It was Thanksgiving, 1971 . . .

My brother, Lou, two-and-a-half years younger than I, had invited me to visit his apartment on the lower east side of Manhattan before traveling together to Long Island for a Thanksgiving meal with our parents. They would eat traditional turkey and we would insistently eat only the vegetables. Our parents thought we were being rebellious, but had tolerated this new fad of ours. The previous spring, while in my freshman year of college, we had both learned a popular form of meditation. Lou and I enjoyed sitting silently, and we had become ardent vegetarians, too. Of course, this was much to the displeasure of our father, who owned a wholesale fish dealership in the Fulton Fish Market on the southern tip of Manhattan.

I walked up the three flights of stairs of the dilapidated dwelling, a stark contrast to the upper-middle class home in which my brother and I had grown up. I knocked on the door at the head of the stairs, and a tall young man answered. In spite of my grave doubts, he confirmed that this was indeed my brother's place.

I could smell a flowery essence wafting toward me from the interior, and I could hear the strangest music, music so joyous that it filled me with a feeling of sheer delight. I danced into the apartment, moving in little circles, Jewish-style, hands held high above my head. Reaching my brother's bedroom, I greeted him:

"Hi Lou!"

He was sitting on the floor on a mat, which I was startled to learn he called his bed, and burst into laughter at seeing me so happy (a strange occurrence), doing an even stranger dance into the middle of his room.

"What are you doing?" he asked.

I enthusiastically replied, "I'm so happy I can't help but dance. This music is wonderful! Who is it?"

Lou responded, "Oh, that's Sai Baba singing bhajans."

"Who's he?" I asked.

His reply threw me for a loop: "He's God. He lives in India."

Instantly my dancing ceased. You see, more than ten years earlier, I had terminated my relationship with God. Hebrew school had been a grueling experience in which I alternated between being yelled at by my teachers for not knowing the Jewish prayers, and being struck with bicycle chains after class by older students who had had a little too much of the one-and-a-half hours of frustration twice a week.

In my lifetime, I had not been able to find a single individual who, in speaking about God, and directing me in the understanding of my religion, had been able to represent it without representing a tradition of anger, selfishness and general pettiness, as well. So how could God exist when there was so little love in my life? Besides, what about the Jews during World War II? So, if God did exist, I didn't like him anyway; and besides, how can a person be called God?

That's where I found myself after dancing into my brother's apartment on Thanksgiving day, 1971. There was too much sorrow in my life to acknowledge God's existence, much less his love, which seemed not to be coming my way. Besides, the holocaust was a good rationalization for my atheism. And, if that wasn't enough, since I was Jewish, God was without form and was certainly not a man.

With no thanksgiving and an arrogant laugh I retorted: "God! What God? The one in your fantasies? Come on!"

My arrogance was no doubt the fruit of an educational career long on "intellect" but sadly lacking in moral training. And I could feel anger rising in me, the anger felt in childhood—born of sadness, loneliness, friendlessness, of not loving, not being loved, not understanding and not being understood.

Lou's response hit me right where my stubborn intellect was most vulnerable:

"See for yourself. Read about him."

That Hanukkah (or Christmas, if you like; my brother believed in Jesus, too) Lou gave me the book *Baba* by Arnold Schulman. Within a few days, I reluctantly opened it and read. After ten pages, I put the book down, my mind numb. In fact, my mind seemed to have stopped—an impossible occurrence, especially for me. After a few all too brief moments, it began again but all I could think was: "Oh, my God! This is God!" In a state of sheer excitement I picked up the phone and dialed my brother.

"Lou, you're right! This is God! Sathya Sai Baba is God! What do I do now?"

He calmly replied, "Relax. Sit down and meditate. When I see you next, we'll talk more about it. Keep reading."

That was the beginning and, I might add, only the beginning of the magnificent, munificent grace which Baba would shower upon me.

In the following year while reading his books, the ones called *Sathya Sai Speaks: Volumes I, II, III*, etc., in the midst of a treasury of teachings, I came across what I thought was a most practical one for an overworked college student:

> The fruit of action belongs to the actor; therefore, renounce the fruit. Act, but renounce the fruit of the action; dedicate every action to God and renounce all desire for its fruit; call upon God to be the doer of action, and totally and fully, without recourse, renounce every vestige of attachment to the fruit of action.

For that entire week I had been trying to write a final paper in my first and only political science course. We had studied the philosophy and leadership in the American civil rights movement. I had read Frederick Douglas, Martin Luther King, Jr., Eldridge Cleaver, Malcolm X, and innumerable other black political figures. The professor had asked us to write one paper to pull it all together. This was it—the only grade in the course. I set about the nearly impossible task and after a week succeeded in crumpling up more than 20 pages of first-page starts. I was in a panic. How was I to enjoy the Thanksgiving break, which was now upon me, if I had to write this paper?

I resolved to retreat to my brother's apartment, where just one year previously, the joy of God's love had touched my thirsty soul. Thanksgiving eve I sat down, paper on desk, pen in hand, and lit a candle before a picture of Sai Baba. I prayed. "Oh, God, hi! It's Al Levy calling. Can you please write this paper on black political thought for me? You are the doer of all deeds, the speaker of all words, the thinker of all thoughts. Please then, write this paper and bear the fruits. I surrender it all to you. Thanks."

For the next sixteen hours or so, he wrote. Every time I seemed to reach an impasse, I called on Baba again for help, praying as I had done before.

The paper was typed the following week at college and handed in. Just before Christmas I received it back. The professor had written, "This is a good paper. You have a nice flow of language. When you talked about Martin Luther King, I heard Martin Luther King talking; when Frederick Douglas was mentioned, it sounded like Douglas was speaking; and when Malcolm X was referred to, it was like him speaking. A job well done. 'A.' "

Of course it was a job well done—by Baba. He had brought the essence of these courageous leaders who had actually left the earthly plane, and had placed their thoughts and words directly into this paper. Thank you Baba!

Through the next thirteen years of my educational experience, I called on my Sai Baba to do the work and bear the fruits. With his grace, I passed through the bachelor of arts degree in psychology and a master's of science in social work from Columbia University. Receiving professional training in psychoanalysis was difficult, but he took me through the Philadelphia School of Psychoanalysis and on to a graduate university where, once more, I prayed to make it through the program.

When I entered this doctoral program in psychoanalysis, the university had not yet been accredited, but the dean assured us it would be, and that all degrees would be retroactively honored with full accreditation status. I decided to enroll.

While engaged in doctoral study, I was offered an opportunity to pass through the program in one year, contingent upon writing an original doctoral thesis on a psychoanalytic topic. They said my previous graduate training qualified me for such an opportunity. Doctoral programs are notorious for being brutally arduous and terribly torturous, taking five to ten or more years to complete. Delighted by the opportunity to be free of the entire educational rigmarole, of which I had been a prisoner for more than 25 years, I took the university up on their one-year offer.

I prayed to my Baba as always, "Please, dear Baba, write this doctoral thesis. Baba, you are the doer of all deeds, the speaker of all words, the thinker of all thoughts. Please, my Father-Mother God, write this paper and bear the fruits too. Thank you." (I had matured a little in my relationship with God by now, so I left out the "Oh, God, hi! It's Al Levy calling" part. I just figured he knew me by now; I had been in trouble so often and called on him so much for help).

But when the year was up, I had only completed the first half of the reading of references necessary to write the paper. Two years passed. The reading and note-taking were done, but, to my despair, no writing. I kept praying to Baba and hoping against the odds set up by my mind that he hadn't abandoned me. The third year passed and some writing had been done but it was rejected by the doctoral committee. They didn't seem to like my topic: "Psychoanalysis and Meditation." What was I to do? I prayed to do nothing and let my Baba do it all.

Within the next six months the doctoral committee accepted the topic without question: "An Exploration into the Psychoanalytic Treatment of the Meditating Patient." During my psychoanalytic student internship, I had found that some of my patients were meditators and were continuing the practice while undergoing treatment. I decided to study the meditating patients to see if they did better in psychoanalysis than my non-meditating patients.

I continued to pray to Baba; but all along the question kept arising in my mind: "Baba, why, when they gave special permission to complete the degree in one year, is it taking so long?" And I complained, "Each three-month term costs fifteen hundred dollars, Baba. Can't we speed it up a little?"

In June, 1985, after four-and-a-half years, the paper was completed. The doctoral committee approved the thesis with minor revisions; and the next month I received, by my Baba's grace, a letter from the university dean congratulating me on the award of the long-awaited Ph.D. The timing was right! During the previous two weeks all the university students and prior graduates had received a letter from the new dean stating that the graduate school, after twelve years, had received full accreditation by the Midwest Regional Committee of Colleges and Universities, as well as accreditation by the University and College Accreditation Board in America, effective March, 1985.

This was the first "university without walls" program in the United States to receive full recognition. However, contrary to the former dean's assurance, the letter continued, the present dean and faculty were sorry to announce that all graduates who had received their degrees prior to March 1, 1985, would not be entitled to accreditation status, according to the regulations of the Midwest Regional Committee.

"Thank you, God!" I exclaimed. My Baba had saved me from an unforseen tragedy. Had I completed the doctoral program any sooner than the four-and-a-half years it had taken, my degree would not have been fully accredited when received. Baba had done it again; his timing was perfect!

My thoughts go to all of you, all who may be struggling through the cumbersome and sometimes obnoxious task of the educational experience, not to mention the ongoing process of life itself. Pray to the Lord to do all the work and bear the fruits thereof. Keep the faith! For it is true:

"Lord God Almighty, Sai Baba my beloved, you are the doer of all deeds, the speaker of all words, the thinker of all thoughts. I surrender it all to you. Please, then, bear the fruits of all my thoughts, words, and deeds. Thank you, Baba." And add a little "I love you" at the end.

And now, as if awakening from a dream, again I find myself sitting at my desk awaiting the next patient. This remembrance of the past has renewed my faith, has given me hope that in this lost world, the light of love is visible. Nay, not only is the light of love visible, but transformational.

For he has transformed my life from a desperate search for love into a deep desire to give love to others. I have groped in the darkness and found happiness and beauty blossoming in the midst of a struggling humanity. Even more miraculously, my life has turned from concerns of self into a sharing of the burdens of life that others seem to bear. The real value of this life I call "mine" has become the intense desire to respond to the cry of pain from another—my own Self in disguise.

By the grace of God, I love, and in that loving, give; and I pray that the giving be so constant, so deep, that one day, realization of the oneness of giver and receiver—the true nature of being—be eternal in this consciousness.

They say God is omnipresent. Everywhere I look I now see his creation. I see him. Yes, God is very much alive and well, and living in Puttaparthi. And we have found him. We can see his face and live!

May his blessings fill our lives and touch all those we meet.

Your hearts are my home! Swami will safeguard the purity of your heart which is His home. Swami will bless you with His presence, around, beside, behind and before you. Remember three things always: Always serve, wherever you are. Seek chances to help others. Never lose an opportunity to use your skills and enthusiasm for the alleviation of sorrow, pain and distress. Again, do not omit or neglect or postpone your own particular spiritual practice. Above all, have the faith that Swami is with you, at all times and places.

—Sathya Sai Baba

LETTING GO IS LETTING GOD IN

Judy Warner

It was in September, 1984, that I first heard of Sathya Sai Baba. In one sentence I can say: My whole life has changed. I am almost totally devoted to Baba or the God within. How this happened, I don't quite understand, but maybe if I recall some of the events of my life and my experiences with Baba, the understanding will come.

I have spent most of my life developing self-confidence and ego, for as a child I had very little sense of my own worth. I was brought up in New York City in an upper middle class family which was highly competitive. My father was a Supreme Court Judge, my mother, an important and influential person in the United Jewish Appeal, and my brother, a famous television producer. It took me thirty-five years before I realized that I was my self and not the judge's daughter, the producer's sister or some appendage of my family. Finally, at 43, I realized I had everything I wanted: two marvelous, healthy children, an ideal long term relationship, wonderful friends and enough money and success. Yet, there was something still gnawing at me; something deep down inside was missing. I used to say to my friends, "No one will ever feel fulfilled unless he feels a connection with something larger than himself—the Source, God, whatever you want to call it."

In 1983, after completing an enormous effort, co-producing and co-writing the music and lyrics for a musical, I made the decision for the first time in my life *not* to decide what I would do next. Somehow my need to prove myself and my desire for recognition no longer seemed important. However, this was not an easy decision. Actually it made me very nervous, for I would have to wait, be patient and experience the anxiety of not knowing. Instead of diving head first into a new project, I was going to try to trust that something would evolve naturally for me.

A year later I read two books about Sri Sathya Sai Baba: *The Holy Man and the Psychiatrist* and *Avatar*. I became completely entranced with the human values expressed by Sai Baba. I felt his love and a special vibration in any book about or by him. I had already read widely in the field of human consciousness and spirituality. As a matter of fact, by a coincidence (if you believe in coincidences), I had recently started working as a freelance editor with a new publishing company in this exact field. I had read Ram Dass, Muktananda, Paramahansa Yogananda; and they all said many wonderful things, but none had ever moved me like Sai Baba.

When I read, *"Let the different faiths exist, let them flourish, and let the glory of God be sung in all languages and in a variety of tunes"*; and when I learned that, unlike most other gurus, Sai Baba does not accept money, I became very interested in him. However, it was these words of Swami's that captured my heart, for this is exactly what I believed:

> *There is only one religion—*
> *the religion of Love*
> *There is only one caste—*
> *the caste of humanity*
> *There is only one language—*
> *the language of the heart*
> *There is only one God—*
> *He is Omnipresent.*

Less than three months later, on January 10, 1985, a friend and I were on our way to India. We flew to Bangalore, rested a few days, gathered supplies and, excitedly, left for Baba's ashram in Puttaparthi.

The first day at the ashram was really a shock. First of all, I had been assigned a room to myself by the accommodations office, with no furniture, no fan, a bathroom which consisted of a hole in the floor, with a faucet four feet off the ground for washing in cold water. This was not exactly inspiring. Secondly, there was an atmosphere of devotion and reverence that was completely unfamiliar to me. At once I realized that I was there to look inward, and that I would have to detach from all the externals or I wouldn't last another day.

Miraculously, within twenty-four hours I had begun to ignore the austerities and to accept the extremely devotional attitude of some of the devotees. I would learn my way and let them have theirs.

On the second day, my friend and I were out taking pictures. We had one picture left, and Baba came right by us in the car. He smiled at me—a smile that went right into my heart. I felt my heart physically open up. My friend looked at me and saw me grinning from ear to ear. "You're all flushed and radiant. I never saw you look like this before." For a minute, I was totally overcome with the love I had received from Baba. Then I said, "Do you think he was really smiling at me or because you were taking a picture?" I heard myself. I couldn't believe what I had said. "That's what Baba means by the monkey mind," I exclaimed. "I can't believe that after such a powerful feeling I could say that. Unbelievable!" But what a lesson. I felt Baba had taught me the necessity of training the mind to focus, to be one pointed, and this was essential for me because, by nature, I am very analytical. I decided right there to suspend disbelief and every time I was tempted to doubt my experience, I would say, "Sohum," the mantra I had chosen from my readings. It means "I am He."

Darshan means "in the presence of a holy being." During darshan Baba gives his blessing, takes letters and indicates which people are to go into the temple for an interview. In the beginning, I was waiting to see a miracle or to get called for an interview; in other words, I was into expectation and desire. After Baba gave me that huge smile, I felt different during darshan— more able to receive—more open and loving.

At first glance you are
But a small man in an orange robe

Sometimes stern, sometimes smiling
You smiled at me and
Gave me a glimmer of Your radiance
When next I saw You
Love enveloped me and
A tear caressed my cheek
I beg You
Come into my heart and
Show me I am One with You.

Listening to my first lecture at the ashram, I got a very helpful clue. The speaker, an American devotee and ashram resident, said, "Don't spend your time here wondering if Baba is divine; look for the divinity within yourself." How right that felt to me. A miracle would be nice but that wasn't what I wanted. I wanted to feel my connection with God. I believe in God, and I believe in myself and in following my own heart and conscience, but I wanted to feel that my heart and conscience were not mine alone. Daily I wrote letters to Baba which helped clarify my own thoughts about what I wanted.

I also began to think about my life, and I wondered why I seemed to have so many crises. I had lost both my parents before I was 30. My brother had died in a plane crash in 1979. I had had an operation for the removal of a lump on my thyroid in 1975 when I was 35 (it turned out to be benign). I had had an unusually difficult divorce in 1976. AND my children had been in the hospital three times within a year-and-a-half in 1980-81.

I was always a "survivor" in these situation, but I knew deep inside that there had to be a better way to live through these experiences. Yet, perhaps I needed these crises. Maybe they were teaching me to surrender. In fact, it was the night before my youngest daughter's spinal operation, after a year of trying all kinds of techniques to arrest the spinal curvature, and in a state of total exhaustion, that I finally did let go. I actually prayed to something or someone, saying, "There is nothing more I can do. Thy will be done."

What happened was truly incredible: the operation was not only a success—the whole hospital experience was easy. I was able to be supportive and loving without my usual fear and anxiety. This was my first recognition of how God reveals himself, if we truly surrender to him.

In those first days at the ashram, I found bhajans strange. I couldn't sing them in Sanskrit or Hindi, and, even though I had written music myself, I found it hard to relate to them musically. After a week or so, I began to find them pleasing and was able to feel the surge of energy they evoked.

Twice during bhajans I smelled a peculiar sweet fragrance around me. It was the same fragrance I had noticed on two occasions back home while reading the Baba books. I asked the woman sitting next to me if she smelled anything. She didn't. I said, "It smells like vibhuti. Maybe that's what it is." But why this fragrance at home? I remember getting up and looking in the kitchen when it happened but I had found nothing. The woman next to me then said, "That's wonderful. Vibhuti is a sign from Baba to let you know he's with you." After she said that, others told me similar stories.

On that first visit, Baba never took letters from me, nor did he talk to me. However, I must confess that he looked at me quite a few times; and every time he did, I felt my heart opening, releasing a flow of love.

One afternoon at darshan I realized I *was* blessed. Another day I realized that although I wanted an interview, I didn't need one. And most important, I realized that where I chose to put my attention was where I would be: focus was everything. Every day I learned something new, but it wasn't intellectual learning; it was learning from the heart. However, the most wonderful miracle was feeling totally calm and completely at PEACE for the first time in my life. Sure, I have known happiness, but this was a "PEACE that passeth understanding."

After I returned from my first trip to India, I joined the Sai Baba Center in Manhattan and began to enjoy singing devotional songs and doing service. At this point in my life I knew

I needed *satsang*, as Baba calls it—being with others on the spiritual path.

> *You ask me*
> *Is Baba Divine?*
> *How can I answer*
> *When I have barely touched*
> *My own Divinity*
> *That He is*
> *More than a man*
> *I am sure*
> *But to know*
> *He is Divine*
> *I must know*
> *That I am too.*

● ● ●

I returned to India on November 7, 1985, for Baba's 60th birthday celebration. There is no way to describe Baba's love and generosity. He was always outside giving darshan, giving gifts, giving free food for a week and, of course, giving love. Truly, his life is his message.

One morning I awoke with intermittent stomach cramps. I went to darshan but decided I should rest and skip bhajans. However, at five minutes to nine, a friend said, "Come on, let's go. Maybe bhajans will make you feel better."

When I arrived at the temple, all places were filled so I wandered around outside and finally sat down on a stoop next to a lovely new friend of mine from Australia. Not more than two minutes had passed when she said to me, "Oh, they're calling the chair ladies. That's me. Baba's giving out saris. I can't go in with this; will you hold it for me?" She handed me a big straw mat and happily fought her way through the crowds onto the temple grounds.

About ten minutes later, I saw her signaling to me. I thought she wanted her mat back, so I slowly got up to hand it to her when she said, "Let the lady through." She then reached for me and pulled me through the crowd that was ten deep. "Go sit down," she said, "Baba's giving out saris to the Westerners." I was totally stunned, partly from what was happening, but also because I was feeling ill and passive.

Within minutes, Baba was walking directly in front of us. He seemed to be deciding which material and color best suited each person. He had a few plain colored, satiny silk ones left. Would I get one of these? If so, which color would he choose for me? All of a sudden, there he was, directly in front of me. He gently dropped an orange sari in my lap. I was stunned, in awe. It was too much for me to absorb. I could not get over the "non-coincidence" of this event. I thought, "If one friend hadn't said to go to bhajans, and if another hadn't told me Baba was giving out saris, I would not be sitting here now."

One day while we were waiting to go in for darshan, a seva dal (service worker), asked for volunteers to give up bhajans in order to help clear the stadium for the birthday celebrations. So, after darshan, I walked alone to the Hill View Stadium. When I arrived, I walked toward the stage, all the time looking for some Westerners to join. I didn't find any, so I squatted near some Indian women and observed what they were doing. I found myself a sharp stone and, using it like a spade, dug the weeds and stones out of the hard ground in order to make it more comfortable for all those who would be sitting there during the birthday week. For me, it was physically hard work—hard on my hands and hard on my back. But the Indian women were so happy to see me. They asked me all kinds of questions. We spoke and laughed together as best we could, Baba being our shared interest. I felt so happy doing this work among all these accepting, loving faces—all from another world. I was beginning to experience, for the fist time, the joy of service, and then all of a sudden, the women started singing bhajans—bhajans I knew, like "Ganesha Sharanam" and "Shivaya Nama Shiva." I couldn't believe it! At that time I only knew a handful of bhajans—which never seemed to be sung at the temple, and now, here I was, able to sing along with everyone. My joy was complete.

I was, once again, convinced that Baba had arranged this experience especially for me—service was one of the best spiritual practices for this upper middle class city "sophisticate."

Around mid-November, as the crowds began to grow, I knew I had to watch myself; it would be easy to become irritated and angry because of the mere numbers of people. Twice I did lose my self-control; and there was a third time, with the crowds at over a half a million people, when I couldn't move at all—not forward or backward or to either side. Everyone was pushing. I cried, "*Shanti, shanti,*" but no one would listen. I became really frightened because there were moments when I was lifted off the ground from the sheer pressure of the crowd. I was desperate; I had to do something—but what? I thought of Baba, and crazy as it may seem, I began to sing, "Shivaya Nama Shiva." Only one man joined in; but, miraculously, a tiny space opened up and I slipped through to safety.

On the morning of November 17th, Baba gave his valedictory discourse in the enormously crowded Poornachandra Hall. When Baba spoke, and the translator translated, I could understand—nothing. Then, all of a sudden, it didn't matter because I could actually feel Baba's voice melting my heart. Was it the gentleness, the tone, the vibration? At no other time was I able to experience this profound feeling. I wondered then if understanding mattered; after all, I could always read the discourse later. If I could feel my heart melting, what more could I possibly want?

My final highlight of the trip occurred on November 22nd, after the overseas devotees had sung to Baba. I was in the chorus and I was very close to the stage. When Baba left in his car, I waved to him, and guess what? He waved back. I was totally overcome. For the first and only time in my life, I experienced universal love: I loved everyone. I don't know how to explain this intense and expansive feeling, but it does exist. This euphoria must have lasted in all its strength for about half an hour and then gently subsided.

The feelings evoked by these experiences have not remained, and yet because they were so powerful, I long to repeat them. I want to live in PEACE, BLISS, UNIVERSAL LOVE, and SERVICE. I am grateful that Baba has given me a taste of all of these. As a result of these experiences, I am now beginning to see the world and my life differently: A New York City bus becomes a love bus where passengers offer each other seats and smile at each other . . . people help each other across the street . . . bag ladies and bums no longer seem threatening . . . people talk kindly to one another. Where have all the self-centered, inconsiderate New Yorkers gone? So, I am proving to myself that living by Baba's teachings—"seeing good, hearing good and doing good"—does indeed change my reality.

My life is truly blessed. Baba says, "Be happy," and I am. The practice of Karma Yoga, dedicating all my actions to the Lord, with no eye on the fruits of my actions, has helped me enormously. Because I have been such a goal oriented person, this discipline has relieved me of the outcome, which often meant anxiety for me. Now I am more focused on the process of life; after all, the fruits are not mine, but the effort still is.

I believe now that Baba is divine; I can't tell you quite how or when this crystallized. But most important, I believe we are all divine. It is now up to us to purify ourselves so that we can experience—not just intuit—our own divinity.

Before You came
We lived as victims in a random Universe
Full of fear and separateness
Never knowing why, never knowing who
Never know Sai, never knowing You

Then You came
We learned of our strength in a perfect Universe
Full of Love and unity

Contemplating why, contemplating who
Contemplating Sai, contemplating You.

• • •

It is now almost three years since I read my first book about Sathya Sai Baba. During these years I have become steeped in the spiritual path and its practices. Yet sometimes I have asked myself if I have truly changed or if I am only playing another game and wearing yet another mask? I have heard this referred to as "spiritual materialism," and I have wondered if I have fallen into this trap. But something happened recently which indicated to me that there are changes going on—deep important ones.

In the spring of 1986, a few of us had begun going to a nursing home every Saturday morning. We chatted, painted pictures, gave manicures and sang songs with all who wanted some company. Before entering the home, I always dedicated my service to Baba. Giving up the fruits of my actions seemed to endow me with strength and love.

Most of the patients were in wheelchairs and very sick; few ever returned home. When I first walked down the nursing home corridors, I was horrified to see the patients so drugged. One woman was so old, ill and medicated that she was unable to sit up straight. She was leaning all the way over to one side. As I passed I prayed she wouldn't notice me, but, no sooner had the thought crossed my mind, when she signaled me to her side. Of course I had no choice but to go over to her. In fear, I quickly re-dedicated my deeds to Baba. I listened to her story, which I couldn't comprehend at all because of her slurred speech. I gently stroked her head and left as soon as I could get away without hurting her feelings or showing my own.

After that incident I thought a lot about my attitude. Baba says that we are all God and we must treat all the same. Yet I found, week in and week out, I was spending time only with those patients I felt comfortable with and those who didn't upset me because of their appearance. And I was avoiding anyone who was bossy, angry or difficult for me to look at. It took a year before I was willing to face this—not just think about it, but face it and deal with it. I dedicated my service to Baba, and I asked for the strength to see all as God. I also let Baba know in my thoughts that I was ready for more challenge.

And so, one Saturday morning, there I was, happily chatting away with some of the ladies I see all the time, when an unknown man arrived, wheeling a woman into the room—a woman so crumpled, so disfigured that she could not keep her body erect; her head was at the level of her waist and her hands were completely gnarled.

I thought, "I hope I can do her nails and no one else gets to her first." As soon as I was free, I went over and began to talk quietly to the "new" lady. I massaged her gnarled hands and even managed to manicure and polish her fingernails. I don't remember much—only that I was happy and totally engrossed; so much so, that it was only after I had finished that I realized I had never seen her as disfigured, nor had I been afraid. As a matter of fact, what I had noticed was her radiant smile. Somehow, by Swami's grace, I had been able to see beyond her physical form and relate to her whole being. I believe this is what Baba means as seeing the divine in everyone.

Open our eyes
Help us to see
Open our hearts
To love Thee
To love Thee in all
As me, as we, as One

Free us from pride
Help us to be
Free from all fear
To love Thee

To love Thee in all
As me, as we, as One

A LETTER NEVER MAILED
. . . BUT ANSWERED

Dear Baba: September 28, 1987

The honeymoon is over. For two-and-a-half years I was filled with the glow of you. You said, "Be happy," and I was. Then what happened? I'm not sure. I do remember saying to you, "I'm ready for more challenge." As a matter of fact, I've said many things to you, and now, looking back, I realize they all came true. I guess we should be very careful what we pray for.

I asked for "more challenge" and that I have. I asked for less ego and that I have. But I thought that when I had less ego I'd be much clearer about what was right for me; I'd begin to tap into my higher Self. Not true at all. What has happened is, I no longer seem to need to prove myself or to show I'm smart or creative. As a matter of fact, I no longer have a desire to do anything and, given my rajasic personality, this is a scary place to be.

It seems that some other motivation, from deep within, will have to replace the driving force of my old needs and desires. Perhaps this is a necessary step in becoming your instrument— the clearing out of some ego in order to "hear" you. I trust that— sometimes. Other times I feel so uncomfortable in this "no place" that I think I will just get a full-time job or write another show— anything to keep me from despair.

I have read that this stage of hopelessness is connected with surrender. Our patterns have changed and our ego is diminishing; if we could just feel this and get into the pain, a new sense of surrender and peace would follow. Yet, easier said than done.

I have always had resistance to change and to pain. I have always wanted to get through these as fast as possible. It has been very hard for me to accept the idea that we must welcome everything that happens to us, good or bad, knowing it is all the grace of God.

However, now I do have the new tools of spiritual practice and my new core beliefs. I believe in you, Swami, and your unconditional love. I believe that in pain there is growth and I believe this is a necessary stage for me to go through. Yet, I feel farther away from you than ever before; my mind is a mass of rubbish, and my joy seems to have been covered over by my resistance to this process. Baba, I need you to help me let go—to BREAK me so that I can cry, not only tears of pain, but tears of joy and devotion.

Dear Swami, I ask only one thing of you. Stay with me, or rather, let me be aware of your presence throughout the journey of this lifetime; then anything will be welcome.

• • •

In November, 1987, I became a hospice volunteer. I decided to follow my training with the Elisabeth Kübler-Ross five day "Life, Death, Transition Workshop." I knew I had, what Elisabeth calls, "unfinished business." For years I had been saying, "I think my stuffed sinuses are repressed tears." I felt that the more in touch I was with myself the better I would be in helping those who were about to die, as well as their families.

If I had known what went on in this workshop, I would have run a mile. What I heard was incredible. Some people had tried to kill themselves, some were dying of cancer or AIDS, others were abused and molested, one was a Vietnam veteran who had seen hundreds of his buddies killed or mutilated.

Participants got up in front of the group, nearly ninety strong, and dealt in few words and mostly feelings with their issues; expressing their deepest hurts, pains, anger, tears and screams. And it was scary—wondering what would happen once the Pandora's Box was opened! At one point I felt so frightened that I was ready to leave. I prayed to Baba: "If I'm supposed to be here, give me a sign—a real sign—nothing vague or abstract. I want a CLEAR sign." Within a few hours I found out that one of the eight trainers was a Sai Baba devotee!

After a while, I felt less panicky, as it became clear our trainers were highly skilled in dealing with these emotions. After forty people had gone through this process, I began to see that everyone suffers grief, rage and pain, although in varying degrees. We are not different; only the circumstances of our lives are different.

One morning as I sat in meditation, I realized that I could just get up in front of the group and not know why specifically—simply trust. Then once I worked through my paralyzing fear, two thoughts came to mind: I had been setting limits for myself and protecting myself for years; but this wasn't necessary anymore because I no longer had anyone to "stay together" for— my children were grown; I was now living alone. I didn't have to be in charge or in control anymore. What I did need to do was to "let go" and let Swami in.

I remember only fragments of what I said to the group, but the feelings I remember well. First, I dedicated this experience to Baba . . . or I couldn't have done it at all. I told about the deaths in my family and the hospital crises. I said I had always felt an enormous sense of responsibility and had always been the "strong" one; I knew I was full of grief and I wanted to cry, but crying was hard for me. I finally let go of my control and began to cry gently. But I really wanted to sob and let it all out.

I was then asked if I wanted to go into another room and work privately to release more of my grief. There I lay on my back, sobbing as I thought of my mother, father, brother and my children, and how I hadn't been a perfect mother—sobbing out all my grief as each one passed through my mind. Every time I felt stuck I prayed to Baba to keep me open and receive my pain. A few times I wanted to talk, but the trainer said, "No words—just sounds." And I knew that was perfect for me; for while I usually knew, intellectually, what I was feeling, I didn't always allow myself to feel it. And although I had always had a terrible fear of losing control, this time my trust in Baba enabled me to let go.

The pain in the room seemed to get lighter as more people got in touch with themselves. The love and support from the group was absolutely astounding. I felt that I would never be able to judge others or myself so harshly again, so deep had been my sense of empathy and connection with all of them. I was beginning to realize that this was a holy experience.

On the last evening, there was entertainment by the group. All were in a gay mood celebrating their release and empowerment. I, on the other hand, began to regress slowly and to feel frightened and little. At the end everyone was dancing; and I felt very disconnected, weepy and scared. Such feelings were alien to me; I normally feel a sense of confidence and belonging in a group.

I began to cry uncontrollably. I became very scared because I felt powerless; I was a victim, reliving a childhood terror of my father which I had so often felt before I was 11. Previous therapy had put me in touch with this memory, and yet I had never fully expressed the actual fear and pain, the feeling of being a victim. I wondered, would I ever recover and feel strong again? I only knew that Baba was with me; and that my "grief" for the little girl inside—so sad and frightened—was a healing grief; and I realized only by loving her and fully embracing this experience would I be free of my lifelong compulsion to be "responsible and in control."

One evening a few days after the workshop was over, I was feeling very sad, and I remembered that Baba tells us to turn to him. So I went to my altar and began to sing some devotional songs. When I sang:

You are my mother, You are my father
You are my nearest kin . . .

I wept like a child. I sang this song over and over letting
the tears flow. I was truly yearning for God. I felt then that I,
with my little ego mind, didn't really know how to be or how
to love, and that I had to get in touch with Baba, my higher
self. I guess I needed this workshop, even though I felt it was
such a violent form of purification. But I had prayed for all this;
I had prayed for my heart to be broken so that I could weep
tears of joy, so I could surrender, so I could serve with true unconditional love, and so I could be closer to Swami, my higher
self, for I, too, am God.

After much crying (remember how I couldn't cry?), I realized
that I had to forgive myself for being less than perfect, especially
with my children, yet doing the best I could with who I was
and where I was at. Only when I forgive myself will I be able
to forgive others; only then will I be able to let go of my control
and let everyone be just as they are and where they are, and
not try to change them.

I know now what it means when we are told we must welcome the pain, for we must accept it all in order to be whole.
Yet how hard it is to welcome suffering, to always remember
that pain is for the purpose of our spiritual growth. I am so
thankful for my experience with Baba, for I now also know that
there is a place behind all the pains and pleasures of existence
where we are whole and perfect, a place beyond body, mind and
thought.

•••

In this raw state I left for India, in mid-December, 1987.
The night before going to the ashram I was very tense with
worry and longing. I had my 20-year-old daughter with me, and

I was very nervous about what she would think about Baba and the ashram. (She viewed her trip to India and Baba as an anthropological study!) In my heart of hearts, I wanted Baba to capture her as he had captured me; or, at the very least, I wanted her to believe in God. I kept trying to detach from this mania of maya by giving her to Baba, but she just kept returning! Then I realized: if I could not give her to Swami and trust that he had brought her here and would take care of her, it meant that I had no faith in him; and all my sadhana had been for naught. With this realization I burst into tears. I ardently prayed for two things:"Baba, please give me some sign of your love, some recognition when I arrive." And, "Please, let me be able to concentrate on you fully and not be pulled away from you because of my attachment to my daughter."

To say that my prayers were answered would be an understatement. During my first darshan the next day, Baba came over to me and asked where I was from. I was shocked. He had never spoken directly to me before.

"Where am I from?" I said stupefied. "I'm from New York." And in a flash he was gone. I wept quietly, and my daughter gently asked if I was all right.

The following morning at my second darshan, I got into the first row. Baba again asked me where I was from. This time I was prepared.

"New York," I said expecting him to move on.

"How many?" he asked.

"Three," I said.

"Go."

And the next thing I knew, my daughter and I and a friend were going for an interview. My tears flowed in an abundance of joy, gratitude, love and release.

Baba was the perfect host, humoring his guests to make them feel at home. First he made vibhuti for the women. It tasted and smelled fresh from the bakery. Then he spoke for a while, but I was so busy crying that I didn't hear anything until I saw him raise his right hand and say, "All the power is in this hand. This is divine power." Then he asked someone, "What do you want?" Out from his hand came a watch (set at the right time) for a young student and next, a lingam for an Italian woman's sick son. He made a ring for a German man. The ring had Baba's picture on it; Baba passed it around for all to see, asking the man, "Do you want Baba or Jesus?" When the man didn't reply, Swami said, "I know. You want Jesus." He blew on the ring twice, and, lo and behold, the ring now had a picture of Jesus on it.

Every time Baba asked someone what they wanted, I repeated to myself, "I only want love, peace, Self-realization." I kept remembering how Baba says he gives us what we want so that we will want what he has to give, and that is realizing our own divinity. I was also thinking that Baba refers to these miracles as "tinsel" compared to what he could really give us.

Later in the interview, Baba turned to a lady and said, "Where is your japamala?"

"What?" she said.

"Where is your mala?" Baba repeated.

"What?" she said again.

"WHERE IS YOUR JAPAMALA?" we all chimed in.

We were all laughing, when out of Baba's open hand flowed this 108 bead, crystal japamala. It was so long . . . it was so big; it took time to come out of his hand. And it came out so silently. I was truly awed. I don't know what happened, but all of a sudden I wanted a japamala—and badly. Where this thought came from I have no idea. I never even thought about a japamala before nor had I ever used one. I said to myself, "Okay now, get your priorities straight. Do you really want a japamala? No. Remember, you want what's really important: peace, love, to know your Self." It was an uphill battle, but I finally recovered.

These manifestations are marvelous to watch, for they are a constant reminder of a larger reality. But what I remember most is the gentleness and sweetness of Baba's voice and his overwhelming unconditional love. That, for me, was the most striking part.

Swami then spoke to us about making decisions. He said we should ask ourselves: "Is it good? Is it bad?" We should wait and come to a decision—not from the intellect but from our conscience and from our hearts. He spoke about education and how book learning was not enough. We must go past the mind and past the body and follow conscience and intuition.

Baba said to me directly that my mind was a bundle of desires. At first this amazed me because I don't need or desire a lot of things. Then I remembered all my desires of the night before when I had been so anxious about my daughter. He told me that I sometimes use "sharp words" and "too many." How true this is, and yet, I was discovering how easy it is to accept his loving criticism. He also said I was a "good woman."

The atmosphere seemed very gay and light to me. I felt joyful. All of a sudden I asked Baba if I could have his hand-kerchief.

"You want my handkerchief?"

"Yes, Swami."

"Later, when I see you again and speak to you privately."

"Do you mean in another lifetime?" I asked.

Now this may sound bold or rude, but it was said in a light, humorous way. Swami smiled and repeated that he would see me again and talk to me privately. I prayed not to get caught up in this expectation.

Baba rose from his chair, and everyone began to touch and kiss his feet. I remembered that when I first observed people doing this, I had said to myself, "Not me. That's an Indian cus-tom." But now I was beginning to understand the significance of padnamaskar. It means surrender at the feet of the Lord, which ultimately means surrender to yourself. So, with great care I leaned over and timidly kissed his foot.

The last thing Baba did was to give out vibhuti packets, and we all walked out of the interview room over-flowing with Swami's beauty and goodness. Only hours later did I realize that I had not worried about my daughter at all during the inter-view—I had been totally immersed in our sweet Lord.

I figured from then on I would be in the back row and that was fine with me. That afternoon, however, I was again in the first row. Baba came along and looked directly at me and said, "Very, very happy." And once again, I cried, more joyful tears.

This entire trip was full of grace. After spending a month at the ashram, I left for a two week trip around India. When I returned for my last three weeks, my experience was entirely different.

This time I felt very peaceful. I kept silence the day after my return and experienced an incredible sense of bliss during afternoon darshan, bhajans and the period in between. My mind was still chattering away; but, for the first time, chatter became the background and the bliss, the foreground. I decided to continue keeping silence during meals, darshan, bhajans, and while waiting on lines; and to talk only when absolutely necessary. Silence is, of course, encouraged by Baba, and now I can see how much is forfeited by unnecessary chatter. For about five or six days, I didn't need or want any personal attention for I felt a deep inner connection with Baba—like nothing I had ever experienced before. With this deeper connection came an awareness of oneness—there were times when he smiled at someone else, and I felt he was smiling at me, and I was, on occasion, able to feel the joy of others when they were receiving Baba's blessing of padnamaskar.

So the first week back was a beautiful inner journey—no attention, no needs, just bliss from within. And then, guess what? Another interview. This time, a private one. I was totally unprepared. The minute I got called for this second interview, my bliss and inner connection with Swami vanished. As a matter of fact, I was almost mute the whole time, which I know was Swami's doing. Yes, I was still able to cry my tears of joy, but my usually sharp mind was just not there. I seemed to be in another space.

During this interview, one of the puzzling things Baba said to me was "Temper." I gently denied this because I don't get very angry; I usually express my feelings in the moment so that they don't get bottled up. But Swami repeated it: "Temper." He said it sweetly, and I knew if he said it, he must be right.

For the whole day I was driven crazy by this word. Finally, it dawned on me. There was another meaning. And when I found out what it was, I could have cried with joy: it was so perfect, proving, in fact—without a shadow of a doubt—that Baba knew me. Yes, I had forgotten that "temper" also means to make more flexible, to soften as in the tempering of gold.

When the private interviews were over, everyone began taking out photos, books, scraps of paper, cameras or any token for Baba to sign, as a permanent remembrance of him. I was completely unprepared—which seemed to be one of my themes for this trip. (Whatever I expected to happen, never did. And whatever I didn't expect, happened.) I was sitting there rather sadly when all of a sudden I remembered.

"Swami," I asked nervously, "Could I have your handkerchief?"

"Not now," he replied curtly.

And then in a complete change of mood, his eyes twinkling playfully, he picked up his handkerchief and feigning anger, threw it at me as if appeasing a child. My heart melted and I quickly tucked the handkerchief next to my breast.

When Baba stood up, indicating that the interview was coming to a close, there was a special moment for me that I will replay in my mind and heart forever. It was a moment where Baba showed that he knew me. Baba had been with me during that Kübler-Ross workshop, while I was rediscovering the little girl inside me and learning to open up to pain; while I was beginning—just beginning—to surrender to him. Yes, Baba knew exactly what I needed. I was sitting right in front of him, and I asked for padnamaskar.

"Here, take," Swami said as he stood up. He patiently waited as I blissfully kissed both feet.

Then as he turned away from me, with his basket of vibhuti packets in hand, I quietly said to him, "I love you Baba. You are my mother and my father."

He slowly turned back to me and with the love of a thousand mothers said, "and you are my daughter."

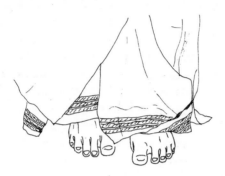

Just as a loving mother cares for her child, if one has surrendered his life to God with full faith in Him, the Lord takes care of that devotee; no need to worry about anything.

—Sathya Sai Baba

OPEN OUR EYES

Words and Music by
Judy Warner

1. OP-EN OUR EYES   HELP US TO   SEE   OP-EN OUR HEARTS   TO
2. FREE US FROM PRIDE   HELP US TO   BE   FREE FROM ALL FEAR   TO

LOVE THEE   TO   LOVE THEE IN   ALL   AS   ME   AS   WE   AS
LOVE THEE   TO   LOVE THEE IN   ALL   AS   ME   AS   WE   AS

1. ONE   2. ad lib. ONE   TO   LOVE THEE IN   ALL   AS

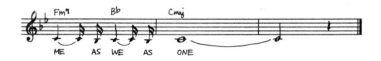

ME   AS   WE   AS   ONE

DESCENDING OF THE HOLY SPIRIT
Pauline Kirby

There is one particular Eastertime that is clearly imprinted on my mind: Good Friday of Holy Week, April, 1977. It was an Easter season that transformed my life. I had an overwhelming experience which finally awakened me from a deep spiritual sleep, a sleep I had been in for years. It changed the way I saw and experienced the world.

I was on my holiday from teaching nursing in the university and had spent my Easter vacation at a very beautiful place, Esalen Institute, on the Pacific coast in Big Sur, California. For five days while attending a seminar at Esalen, I found myself inexplicably immersed in thoughts and images of the Christ story. I say "inexplicably" because I thought I had long since abandoned my Christian roots and freed myself from all religious fetters. But now, for the first time in many years, many warm remembrances of those childhood Bible stories were filling my consciousness and bringing with them a profound joy and inner peace. I had planned to spend the last two days of my vacation quietly returning home to the Sacramento Valley; however, some inner prompting invited me to stay on one more night in this lovely setting to continue to experience my own calmness.

When I went to the office to arrange for a room for another night's lodging, I was told there was no room in the inn. I remember feeling a little bit like Mary and Joseph when they were looking for a room in Bethlehem. But almost as soon as I walked out of the office, I ran into a warm, friendly soul living there. In the course of our conversation she offered me her extra room, if I wanted to stay over!

Next I went to purchase a meal ticket and was told there were no meal tickets available. The place was already crowded, and there were more people to feed than food. I then remembered that it was Good Friday, and this was the day Christ had suffered on the Cross to save mankind. I certainly could forgo one meal on this holy day, but even this was not to be. When I went into the dining room to get a cup of tea, a friend handed me a plate of food. It seems that the cosmos was making sure that I was being totally cared for, just as Mary and Joseph had been at the time of the nativity.

What a strange course of events. Here I was, a fallen-away Catholic spending so much time thinking about Christ. I had grown up in a very strict Catholic family and had always been very devout until I graduated from college. Very shortly after graduation, I quit going to Mass and decided that Catholicism was no longer right for me. I could no longer agree to follow blindly the religious rituals when they were not providing any meaningful inspiration for me in my new life as a career woman. I even decided to give up on God. I remember throwing out my college Bible which I had used in many theology classes. I felt so certain that there would be no further need for it in my life.

Well, it was now eight years later; and as I was looking out at the beautiful Pacific Ocean, I found myself contemplating on how Jesus had spent his time in the Garden after the Last Supper. I remember being aware of how he had known all that was to happen, and yet had allowed the drama to be enacted because of his overwhelming love for mankind.

After spending a very lovely evening in atunement, for the first time in many years, with God and nature, I retired to my room. It just so happened that this particular room had a skylight so I could look up and gaze at the beautiful star-lit sky. I quietly got into bed, after arranging to sleep directly under the window, and began to relax and reflect on all the wonderful events of the past week.

I looked up at the skylight; and suddenly a star started coming down from the heavens. It streaked across the sky getting brighter and brighter and continued right on through the window, entering directly into my room. It was awesome. I was utterly stunned and amazed.

I must explain that I do not use intoxicants, and I have never had visions, hallucinations or unusual imaginings. I was really a fairly conservative college teacher; this was completely outside my realm of experience. At first I was truly frightened; but then the wistful children's story of *Pinocchio* flashed across my mind—when the star came into Guiseppe's shop and all the wooden toys began to do the dance of life.

Almost instantaneously, my room shone with a very strong light. Everything seemed so clear and beautiful. It was totally overpowering. I was in a complete state of awe and wonderment. I remember saying, "Is this happening to me? Is this a dream? Am I asleep?" But I was totally awake and my mind was perfectly clear. Yes, it was really happening!

The star then began to flash various streams of light, and as these flashed before my eyes, I heard a very loving voice giving me clear directions about my life. The messages were very simple, and there was no doubt in my mind that this was guidance from above. One of the first things this sweet voice said was, "You need to give up sugar, particularly coca cola."

I must say this star knew me well. My usual habit was to spend the mornings in the hospital supervising students and then rush back to the university for my afternoon lecture class. On the way to class, I would stop at the vending machines and buy one candy bar and two coca colas. That was my lunch. I knew that this was not good, but it seemed I needed God's loving intervention before I could change.

The voice also told me to become a vegetarian, become celibate, and begin to worship God. Later, when I came to Sai Baba, I realized that these were his exact teachings. The star then told me I was to come and live at Esalen Institute in June and to begin to study natural medicine. It told me not to worry about my job, my house or anything. All my needs would be met. This was truly astonishing because I had been very interested in alternative healing methods. I also had been wishing for some way to leave the traditional health setting. Here again,

I found myself receiving direct orders from the divine, fulfilling a deep inner desire.

The star stayed with me for quite some time. The flashes of light and the voice all happened in a very synchronized pattern, like an orchestra playing a symphony around the cosmic dance of life. Everything was noticed and given its full attention; not a single note was missed. I was totally engrossed in this all-inspiring experience—there was nothing to compare it with; it was beyond all that had been previously known to me. I remembered the picture of Mary appearing to the three children of Fatima; this image was the closest I could come to grasping an experience of this magnitude. Yes, I realized there really is a God, and he is directing every move of my life. To have this knowledge gave much comfort to my disenchanted heart.

Some time during the star's presence, I remember feeling very afraid, and immediately the image of climbing up and down stairs came into my mind. To me, go down meant to descend into darkness and the unknown, while to go up meant to follow the light and learn what the real truth is. I now realize how similar this insight was to the Asatoma prayer of Sai devotees:

Lead me from the unreal to the real;
Lead me from darkness to light;
Lead me from death to immortality.

Even then Baba was imparting one of his essential teachings, and I now pray that he will lead me in my continuing climb to him.

After the star left, I got out of bed feeling completely overwhelmed. I was so filled with energy that I knew there was no way I was going to sleep, so I decided to go for a walk. I made my way down to the rocks on the beach, and it was there that I was able to first realize the true significance of this event. As I gazed out on the ocean, I looked up into the sky and immediately saw two white birds flying over my head. They looked very much like white doves. On seeing these white birds, my thoughts wandered back to the sacrament of Confirmation in the Catholic Church. It is taught that when one receives this sacrament, the grace of the Holy Spirit enters your body, and you become a full disciple of Christ. And what is the symbol of Confirmation? It is the dove!

During my Catholic upbringing, I had memorized all the answers in the catechism book so that I would be well prepared for any questions the bishop might ask me at my Confirmation ceremony. As a 12-year-old, I had looked forward to this occasion with much anticipation and eagerness, the finalizing of my commitment to Christianity.

In my parish church, in a small Nevada town, Confirmation only happened every two years. This was a big event involving many preparations, rehearsals and other doings. The bishop came; I answered his questions perfectly, was anointed on the forehead with the sacred oil and was supposedly accepted as a disciple of Christ. Yet, I walked away feeling empty, knowing that nothing significantly had changed inside myself. I remember thinking: it is just a chance to get a new dress, some presents, and have a big celebration. What was the real significance of all this ritual? It must have some meaning, but I was disappointed and disillusioned at the emptiness I felt.

Well, approximately twenty years later, unexpectedly, on that Good Friday night on the California coast, I suddenly realized I had truly received my sacrament of Confirmation. Here was the experience I had longed for as a child. I now knew without any doubt that the Holy Spirit had entered my body. After being completely alienated from my religious beliefs for eight years, I was experiencing the same feeling that Christ's apostles must have felt when the Holy Spirit descended on them forty days after Christ rose from the dead. I was now one of the apostles.

I vividly recalled the account in the Bible, of Paul's journey to Damascus, when suddenly a light appeared before him and a voice spoke to him from above. He was so awe-struck that he immediately converted to Christianity, and from that day on, he dedicated his life to spreading the message of Christ to all parts of the world.

Yes, I was one of the apostles. I was now Paul.

The way Baba chose to reveal his divinity to me was an awesome experience that I now realize was designed uniquely for my eyes. My given name is Pauline, and therefore my patron saint is Saint Paul. It is no wonder that I should first be made aware of his divine presence through an experience with light. How special we are to him is evident in the dramatic way he individualizes our experiences so as to lead us to his divine lotus feet.

The next morning I returned home with a whole new understanding of God. I started following the directions of the star explicitly. One of the first things I did was to look for my old theology notes from college. It was at this point I remembered throwing out my Bible and thought to myself, "Oh how foolish I was to think I could throw God out of my life." I knew then that he was totally with me and that there was no way I could live in this life without experiencing God. I decided I needed a new Bible, so I went to the bookstore to purchase one. There were many different versions, but the version I had studied so hard in college was not to be found. A few days later, I was in a place where there happened to be some used books for sale. Immediately my eyes fell upon an exact replica of the Bible that had been mine during college. I quickly purchased it, very happy that my old friend was now back in my life.

Since the star had told me to come live at the institute in Big Sur, I immediately began to make plans. I applied and was accepted for a three month work study program. I completed my teaching assignment at the university and prepared my courses for the fall semester so that someone else could easily carry on my duties. I was sure I would not be returning.

I arrived in Big Sur the first of June and at once felt a complete sense of well-being that affirmed my new direction in life. Very shortly after my arrival, I discovered that there was a Catholic Hermitage only eleven miles from the institute. I began attending Mass regularly and felt completely at home in this cloistered environment. I remember walking into the chapel for the first time and knowing that I was returning home after a long absence. The monks were very kind and simply treated me as a fellow spiritual seeker. They seemed to be completely open and accepting of a vast range of spiritual paths—a strong contrast to my very rigid religious upbringing.

Approximately two weeks after my arrival at Esalen Institute, I heard of a morning meditation period I could attend, which was followed by a bhajan session. This was my first exposure to Sai Baba. I think he captured me with those bhajans. I just loved singing them; it was very reminiscent of singing Latin in the choir when I was a child. I did not know the Latin meanings of those hymns, and here again, I found myself not knowing the meaning of these Indian songs. However, the sounds simply captured my heart.

Soon I started reading about Sathya Sai Baba. The very first book I read, called *Vision of the Divine*, disclosed Swami's trademark, TPS, inscribed on a medallion which he had materialized. It means Tara (star), Puttaparthi in the form of Sathya. Then I realized it was he who had come as that wonderful star; it was he who had descended into my world on Good Friday night; it was he who had completely changed my life. Before long I would embark on my first trip to India to experience directly his divine human form.

After my trip to Swami, and on returning to Esalen to continue my studies as a natural healer, I now knew that there was a God incarnate who was directing and guiding my life. Of this I had no doubt. Early on at Esalen, I began studying a variety of natural healing methods with a teacher who "happened" to be also a devotee of Sai Baba. He had acquired a wide knowledge of natural healing methods including acupuncture, homeopathy, rolfing, massage, herbology and nutrition. I learned many things, but I became particularly attracted to acupuncture and homeopathy. Soon, I was assisting him with the Esalen acupuncture and natural healing clinic.

One day I happened to be giving an acupuncture treatment to a famous anthropologist, a person who had visited Baba a few times, when a friend of his arrived. His friend happened to be the Governor of California at that time. After I finished, the Governor asked me where I had learned acupuncture and if I was licensed. He then told me that he had just signed a law stating that acupuncture could be learned by the tutorial method. He said that I would probably qualify and that I should start going to the acupuncture committee board meetings.

Actually, for over a year, I had been attending these meetings, but they were still developing guidelines for the tutorial program. I had already applied, giving them a complete report of my studies, but they had not responded to my application.

A very important committee meeting had been scheduled in Los Angeles on the same weekend that a Sai Baba retreat was scheduled to take place outside of San Francisco. I was in a real dilemma: which to go to? I really did not want to attend the meeting in L.A.; the meetings were boring; it was a very long drive, and the committee might not even talk about the tutorialships; but most of all I wanted to go to the Sai retreat in San Francisco.

On Wednesday of that week, I still had not decided what I was going to do. I called up the board to find out if the tutorial applications were going to be discussed and was informed that the meeting had been moved to a San Francisco location! Now I could do everything I wanted. As always, Baba had shown his omnipresent hand in removing all obstacles. So off I went to the meeting, where I learned that my application had been approved and that I would be allowed to take the acupuncture examination.

With Swami's divine intervention, I passed the exam and received my license. As I look back, I realize that my "achievement" was indeed Baba's grace: The star had told me to come to Esalen and become a natural healer; I had followed my star and was not only blessed to receive all my training free, but also to become the first person to be licensed under the tutorial program.

Swami proceeded to further my acupuncture education by allowing me to study in China. In early 1981, I had decided I would like to take a three month course in acupuncture in Beijing. I applied and was accepted for the Fall course. Approximately a month before I was to go, I decided that the course was too expensive; I would ask Beijing to permit my enrollment to be postponed until the Spring of 1982, in case I decided to go then. During that Fall of '81, I was thinking about taking a six month leave from Esalen and either going to China for three months and India for three months or spending the whole six months in India. I was debating what to do when one day the co-founder of Esalen asked me approximately how much it would cost for me to go to China. I told him, and he immediately offered me a $5000 grant from Esalen that would enable me to make this trip to China. Once again, I felt Swami's divine hand guiding my life.

I went to China and had a very educational, enriching experience. I continued my journey to India where I ended up staying six-and-a-half months. During this extended time in Swami's presence, I became steeped in his divine love and his basic teaching of truth, right action, peace, love and non-violence.

I know now that when the star visited me on that holy night of Good Friday, I not only received the Holy Spirit and became a disciple of Christ, but also became a part of a much larger family—that of all mankind; all of whom are soon destined to receive the Holy Spirit. The father of this world family is our beloved Sri Sathya Sai Baba, who is God once again incarnate in human form to spread his divine love. He has promised us that he will bring this troubled earth of diverse religious streams, cultures and hostile factions back together again in love, united in one family. He gave us a wonderful view of this world family when he said:

There is only one religion,
                    the religion of love
There is only one language,
                    the language of the heart
There is only one caste,
                    the caste of humanity
There is only one God,
                    He is omnipresent.

That is the true Communion, the holy union of the Father, the Son and the Holy Spirit within us, that we are all praying for. May he bless the world to experience the Golden Age very soon.

Flying hither and thither, higher and higher, the bird has at last to perch on a tree for rest. So, too, even the richest and most powerful man seeks rest, peace. Without peace, life can be a nightmare. Peace can be got in only one shop: inner reality. The senses will drag you along into mire, which submerges you deeper and deeper into alternative joy and grief; that is to say, prolonged discontent. Only the contemplation of unity removes fear, rivalry, envy, greed, and desire— all the feelings that prompt discontent, and grant unruffled peace. Every other avenue can give only pseudo-contentment.

—Sathya Sai Baba

IN THIS LIFETIME

Dorothy Herron

As I recall those life events that occurred before Sathya Sai Baba brought me to him, I now see a unifying thread—a harmonizing purpose of which I was unaware at the time.

My story begins with memories of early years spent with a great-aunt and uncle. Having lost a daughter years before, and never having another child, they had persuaded my mother to allow me to live with them. At the time I went to live with my aunt and uncle, I was two-and-a-half; they were in their fifties—"elderly" in those days—and very protective of me. Consequently, I had no childhood friends, not even from the many church gatherings I attended with them.

My one great love and constant companion at this early age was Jesus. He was very real for me. I loved him very much. For me, Jesus symbolized a sunlit garden filled with all the goodness that ever existed in one's heart.

I lived with my great Aunt and Uncle until I was 7 or 8, when my Uncle died. At that time arrangements were made for me to return home to my family. I returned to find I was the second to the eldest child; there were three younger children and another was soon to be born. Like most young children I made a quick adjustment; but in the process of becoming united with this large family, I lost my deep connection with Jesus. Many times, from age 7 to 12, I went to church, but the close relationship I had felt, when I was small and alone, and had relied solely on Jesus, was never to be the same again.

I stayed with my family until my marriage at age 18. Right away I had two children—and I would spend the next twelve years as a housewife and mother. All this time I was an atheist, but I was always looking for truth.

In my adult years, the first event that made a powerful impression on me was the assassination of John F. Kennedy. It was so difficult to believe something like this could happen.

From that time onward, I became politically active and began to relate to a larger viewpoint of the world. Throughout the '60's, I placed a great deal of value on making a political commitment, joining a liberal Democratic organization because I felt they cared more for all people. With this new-found consciousness I worked in many election campaigns in an attempt to make a statement with my life.

At that time I was raising two teen-agers and helping to run a moderately successful business. My life was very comfortable; however, my new political views were not shared by my social circle and my family, and I began to feel a separation and a questioning of my values. There did not seem to be enough depth to my life.

I used to think, "If only I could know some ultimate truth"; but nothing I found provided a satisfactory answer. I used to question lots of people on their beliefs in God because I wanted to know if they truly believed. In all my attempts, I never met anyone who spoke from the heart. For many, God appeared to be a principle to accept unthinkingly, but not a motivating force in their lives; this was not enough for me.

When I was 41, I had to undergo surgery for a tumor which attending doctors thought might be malignant. Fortunately, there was no sign of cancer, but I had a slow recovery. In the early months of getting my strength back, I knew my life had to change. I knew if I were to live another twenty years, I had to have another kind of existence.

Nothing was clear to me—I was in a crisis. I considered divorce. It seemed as if my husband and I were going in different directions, and divorce offered a way for me to be alone and listen more closely to my own thoughts and feelings. But my children still had to complete their college years. No, I couldn't do it. Not yet.

It was at this time that I started studying astrology. I found I had an intuitive understanding of the principles of consciousness which the planets represented. Another interest was reawakened at this time. As a teenager, I had read many books about India, mostly the works of the Theosophists. Somehow, India always held a fascination for me; it seemed that the yogis knew a mystery, and I wanted to learn about that mystery.

I began to feel that I had found a key to understanding what was going on inside of me. As I worked with people's astrological charts, I became aware of mandalas or objects of meditation which expressed unity and a sense of harmony and wholeness which was new to me.

During those years of study I began to sense a larger dimension to people's lives. This proved to be a very healing force in my own life. For the very first time in my adult years, I began to think seriously about God, because I could now see that events were not random. There was order, and I could experience it. I had always believed in reincarnation; and now my studies in astrology appeared to confirm this belief.

When I was 44, with 25 years of marriage behind me, I realized my husband and I had given our best to try to work things out, but it was not successful. I sought a divorce. My life became more difficult. I returned to college, eventually bought the family business and somehow managed to keep things going while I was in the process of personal discovery.

At this time, something or someone called me to the Ramakrishna Vedanta Temple. I began to study Indian philosophy in earnest, and I experienced a spiritual awakening which gave rise to a sense of peace and a belief in God. My new-found belief was not Christian; it did not have a form . . . yet. It was a faith that God and our world exist in a harmonious relationship. I began to feel more creative and expansive.

Little by little this miracle of my faith began to penetrate to a deeper place, forming an inner core that steadied me in times of crisis. I began to trust. It still had no name, no particular teacher—only an expanding sense of the unity of all creation.

After three years of study with Swami Chetanananda, I asked if I could come and talk with him. It was July, and this was the first time I had ever thought of discussing my doubts. I told him I did not feel Ramakrishna was the real guru for me,

or that he was an embodiment of God. What I did not say was
that after reading the *Visions of Ramakrishna*,[1] I seriously doubted
the saint's sanity. Ramakrishna's deep mysticism, so touching to
me now, was only disturbing to me then.

Swami Chetanananda was very reassuring; he told me not
to worry: when the time was right, I would find my guru.

A month later on my way to a weekend vacation, I stopped
to buy a book to take with me. While looking over the titles,
I saw *The Holy Man and the Psychiatrist*. My mind took this in
and thought: "Hmmm, this might be interesting . . . an American
psychiatrist who went to India and became a holy man!" (Sathya
Sai Baba did not look like an Indian to me—I thought he was
an American.)

I purchased the book, packed it in my bag, left that night
for a two day stay in Santa Barbara. Next morning at 8:00 A.M.
I opened the book over breakfast, and at noon I was still reading.
Oblivious to the passing hours, I had made a profound discovery—I knew in my heart that Sathya Sai Baba was God.
Though my mind was still in the stage of inquiry, my heart had
been convinced.

None of the various diversions I had planned for this vacation now held any interest; I packed and returned home.

The first thing I did was to call my sister who had shared
the spiritual quest with me.

"Patt," I said. "I think I've found something really real." I
told her about the book and urged her to go get a copy. She
did read it and had exactly the same reaction.

Shortly after this, Patt went to a Sai Baba center and spoke
with one of the members, Dick Bock. He invited us to come
attend a bhajan singing group on a Friday night and to enjoy
the satsang. We did; it felt so right to us that we began to attend
regularly.

---

[1] Swami Yogeshanda, *Visions of Ramakrishna* (Hollywood, CA: Vedanta Press, 1974).

We also contacted Elsie Cowan after reading about her husband's resurrection. She invited us down to share her experiences of Baba with us. She also opened up the book center, which was next door to her at the time, and showed us many pictures. I bought a full-size picture of Sathya Sai Baba standing in front of some beautiful bushes in Prasanthi Nilayam. That picture seemed to be full of sunlight, just like my childhood image of Jesus. It is framed and hangs over my bed, still so full of the promise of beauty and love.

Patt and I, like all new devotees, could not read enough, learn enough, talk enough or speculate enough about Sathya Sai Baba. Nothing else mattered. I set up an altar in my apartment and spent most evenings there. I was happy; I really felt that Sathya Sai Baba was the heart of my heart.

We did not go to India until 1979, but once we finally made the trip, we received a royal welcome: at darshan other devotees placed us in the very first row; Swami came right up to us and smiled and blessed us. We had brought him roses. He touched them and made us feel so warm and accepted. At that time we did not realize how much this meant; only later would we understand the depth of the blessing Baba had given us.

The following year we journeyed to India again to have his darshan. I felt loved as I had never been loved before. When I returned home, someone suggested that I might like to work with the Bal Vikas children at our center. I volunteered and quickly found that I loved the work.

There was one little boy, around 5, whom I became particularly fond of. He would often fall asleep, and he seemed to be more anxious than the rest of the children. My heart went straight out to this child, and each week I would prepare a lesson plan that in some way would reassure this sweet-faced boy that things were really okay.

From the beginning, I was happy as a Bal Vikas teacher, and I was eager to share with these children what I was learning about Sathya Sai Baba, Indian culture, and all the many treasures we were experiencing here and now in our awareness of the divine incarnation.

In the summer of '81 I was chosen to attend the first over-seas conference for Bal Vikas teachers at Prasanthi Nilayam, I felt uncertain and unqualified because I was not an accredited teacher. I knew I had to go to represent our center since we had a very active Bal Vikas program. I was at the ashram for six or seven days attending classes every day; and Baba came and spoke with us, or just came to listen. This was an inspiring experience; everything we were learning and hearing from these educators confirmed my own views about education for children. To this day I still value a small notebook full of notes gathered at this conference.

When I returned from India in September, I picked up my life anew but somehow I was different. I had been very sick in India and had received injections for ten days in order to recover. The doctor who had treated me was a very learned scholar on Vedanta and he had spent hours talking to me about God. He later became a devotee of Sathya Sai Baba. I shall always feel Swami sent him to help me. During the illness I had a dream of Mother Kali in which she told me that she must purify me and this would hurt. At the time I was too ill to really care if I lived or died; but now, in looking back, I realize my dream of divine mother really did have great inner significance.

When I returned to teaching the children, the first time I heard the sloka, "Guru Brahma, Guru Vishnu," I dissolved in tears. I did not know what was wrong. Tears would come when-ever I looked deeply at a picture of Swami, or whenever I tried to talk about him.

One day I was writing a story for the children about a squir-rel who lived in my backyard. I named him Timmy, and I told how he lived from day to day thriving on food from all the trees in the yard. One day Timmy lay down and was very sick. For the first time Timmy began to see things differently. When he recovered, he had changed; he now had a deep reverence for all of life. The story ended with Timmy profoundly affected by his experience; he had become a peacemaker in the garden community, living a life of spiritual discipline, and knowing that when he left this life, he would merge again with a light and love now dimly remembered.

Writing this tale of Timmy's transformation struck a deep chord within me; for I realized it was my own story. I was different. Baba had somehow awakened me a little, and I was continuing to change inwardly. None of this was apparent at first but slowly, slowly, painfully, Baba had begun to work on me.

At this time I was asked to take over our Bal Vikas program, and again I felt I was inadequate to this task. I was still a worldly person. I only knew that I loved Sathya Sai Baba and believed sincerely that he was God incarnate. I also loved the children and was inspired by what Sai Baba says about teaching children; so I agreed to take over the program, and this began my real connection with Swami.

At Christmas time I was still uncertain about my capacity to serve as leader of our Bal Vikas program. While singing Christmas carols with the children, suddenly the words became living truths: "Joy to the world, the Lord has come. Let earth receive her king." The tears came like a river; I felt these words in the very depths of my heart. I looked at the picture of Swami on the altar with his upraised hand, and it was glowing golden; and he clearly said, "Why are you worried? You have my blessings." Then I could really not stop crying.

The whole day was an amazing day. Nothing was the same as it used to be. There was a quality of light to everything; it was not in the physical sense, but something else. I was feeling so much love, I could not stop crying or talk about what was happening to me. I just knew that I saw everything with different eyes, and all I could feel was how beautiful life was; there seemed to be unity at the heart of all; and we were all joined in love. This revelation lasted all day. I have never forgotten the events of that day; it was the first time that I had such an overwhelming, direct experience of Swami's loving grace.

All this happened back in 1981. Since then I have had so much inspiration for our Bal Vikas program; I know it is not me. I could never come up with so many ideas for lessons, or the experiences of joy and bliss that continually happen in the program. This is Swami's grace; and I know all the guidance we are receiving comes directly from him. There is an atmosphere of love and harmony which surrounds our Bal Vikas program, and we are all so grateful to Swami.

My life has only one real goal now, and that is to surrender to Swami so I can experience my own eternal connection with him. Whatever happens to me, I try to remember, is what God is doing with this body to bring me to a more perfected state.

Since my return from Sathya Sai Baba's 60th birthday celebration, I am aware that the avatar has allowed us all to incarnate with him. Before, I used to think, "Oh Swami, why did I have to wait so long to come to you again?" Now I realize he allowed me to be born only four years after his advent; and he alone knew when my heart would be softened enough to be able to hear his message of love.

I am so grateful I was called to him in this lifetime to experience the healing within my heart through his loving presence.

Love, Love, Love! Become what you truly are—the embodiments of Love. No matter how others treat you or what they think of you, do not worry. Follow Jesus Christ. Love for your own evolution and not for what others say. Do not imitate others. Cultivate your own life. You have your own heart, your own opinions, your own ideas, your own will. Why then imitate? Follow your chosen path. Let your own experience of God be your guide and master.

—Sathya Sai Baba

TURNING INWARD
Hugh Brecher

It was in 1975, while attending a workshop, that my wife and I first heard of Sathya Sai Baba. During a discourse on the subject of reality, the leader stated that an Indian Baba had materialized a gold ring for a friend of his. The gold ring was said to have been created from nothing. This first brief and only mention of Baba was a seed, which unknown to us at the time, was later to sprout and grow into the most meaningful quest of our lives.

In 1978, just four months after my wife first saw Sai Baba's picture on a book cover, she was with him in India. My mind didn't know what to make of it all. Although my relationship with Judy called for my total support of her need to be with Swami, still I was frightened, skeptical, jealous and confused.

I harbored scary thoughts of losing her to Baba himself . . . to illness . . . to another man . . . and to the unknown in general. Having read *Man of Miracles* as well as *The Holy Man and the Psychiatrist* and having heard numerous Baba stories from Judy and others, my curiosity and skepticism, not to mention Swami's invisible tug, pulled me to his ashram in southern India in the winter of 1980.

I'd never spent so many hours in an airplane; it seemed to take forever. Although the flight was smooth and uneventful— except for seeing two shooting stars as we entered Indian airspace—I was super-grumpy as we deplaned. Approaching the customs area we were greeted by a customs official. Looking past him I saw what looked like total chaos as hundreds of people stood by sheepishly while the customs agents seemed to be carefully searching all their luggage.

"How was your flight?" asked the customs official.

"Okay," I said, "but I'm really tired; I have a backache and I'm in a very grouchy mood."

He then apologized—although I don't know why—and sent us, luggage and all, right past the luggage examination area. All we had to do was show our passports; not a single bag was opened. "What luck!" I thought. (Or was it, really?)

After an overnight stay at a hotel in Bangalore, we journeyed by taxi to Prasanthi Nilayam, Sai Baba's ashram, adjacent to the village of Puttaparthi. I couldn't believe that the trip from the USA would be worthwhile, especially after seeing and settling into the room that we had been given to use during our visit. Something wonderful would have to happen to me, just as compensation for my learning to adjust to our Indian-style toilet.

My first sight of Sai Baba was unremarkable. He looked like a nice enough man, but a "man of miracles"? I'd have to wait and see. After my first few days, the nicest and "highest" man I had encountered was the rice man in the ashram canteen. After several days I was still skeptical, homesick, and becoming increasingly moody. One beautiful morning my darshan line was sent in first. I would be up close and maybe even get a chance to speak with Sai Baba.

But what should I say? Should I ask for something? I realized that I was carrying a school ring on behalf of a patient of mine, in order to have it blessed if the opportunity should arise. Besides the ring, I had a new sandlewood japamala (prayer beads) which could also be offered for Baba's blessing. My chance was at hand; Baba was about to pass directly in front of me. Now he was looking right at me as he approached.

With the ring and the beads cupped in my outstretched palms I spoke, "Baba, please bless these things."

Swami smiled, put his right hand on top of mine and pressed firmly. He then sang—not spoke—the words: "I bless."

As Swami continued on his way, I was overcome by the strongest and deepest outpouring of emotion that I can recall. It didn't make any sense to me. What was it that overwhelmed me? It is contrary to my nature and my imagined machismo to allow myself to collapse in tears, sobbing uncontrollably in front of other people. I knew that someone like John Wayne just wouldn't behave this way. I was in shock. Still in tears when I met Judy back at our room, I started laughing when she remarked, "Well, it looks like he got you, too." Apparently Judy and other friends of mine noticed a visible difference in my appearance after this episode.

It was Christmas Eve when Sai Baba called Judy and me in for my very first personal interview. Following the gestures of Baba's volunteers, I made my way to the veranda to await his return from the throng of people who were receiving his darshan. I had a backache, was extremely nervous and my mind was racing. To calm my mind and center myself, I closed my eyes and began to use my japamala as I recited the divine names of God. After a little while someone touched and shook my shoulder. As my eyes popped open, I saw Baba standing there beaming at me and saying, "You don't have to do that now. I am here." I was already feeling a lot better. Even my backache, caused by prolonged cross-legged sitting, had disappeared.

Within minutes Swami ushered a group of us into his interview room. As we were seating ourselves facing his red velvet chair, Swami, the perfect host, moved about the room chatting with people and turning on the fan and room lights.

I had been considering the possibility that Baba might somehow be producing his materializations by sleight of hand and wanted to be in a position where I could see up his sleeve. So, of course, I wound up sitting at his right knee with a perfect view. At no time was there anything up his sleeve except for his wrist and forearm.

In the course of the interview Baba produced several items: a golden medallion, a silver necklace with a medal attached, a japamala and a silver box of vibhuti. Some of them appeared in his hand following a circular motion. The medallion, I believe, materialized in the air above his hand, which he then caught before it fell to the floor. My mind immediately created the new mental category of "real magic." Swami's materializations were so impossible that ordinary logical thinking simply did not apply. I did not—and cannot—doubt the reality of these and many subsequent experiences. Swami had totally opened my mind to allow for the truth of "other" existing realities.

At the time of this interview I had been working as a psychotherapist in private practice. To facilitate the communication skills of my clients, I had spent many hours each week helping them to maintain eye contact comfortably. We would sit silently looking into each other's eyes, knee to knee, for increasing periods of time. When the client could do this comfortably for twenty or more minutes, he would "graduate" to a more difficult communication excercise. My own personal skill and comfort with eye contact had thus been enhanced to the point where I had to remember to look away from time to time in the course of ordinary relationships to avoid making other people uncomfortable.

This "eyeball to eyeball" experience would not be specially noteworthy except for what Baba did with me during this first interview. What did he do? Well, again and again, smiling all the while, he bent at his waist while tilting his head to one side and looked into my eyes from a distance of only several inches. He was clearly playing with me. Again and again, between private interviews with others in our group, Swami looked into my eyes from such a short distance that we could have rubbed noses. By this playful little eyeball game Baba lovingly demonstrated that he really knew me and what I had been up to.

In the course of the private interview with Judy and me, Baba continued to shower attention and affection on me. My mind was as quiet as it had ever been while he was answering Judy's questions. While still conversing with her, Swami looked at me, put his left hand on top of my head and said, "I give you peace of mind." A minute later, again interrupting his talk with Judy and touching my head, he said, "I give you prosperity." A short while later, repeating the gesture, Swami gave me the blessing of long life. All I was able to say in response was, "Thank you."

Is it any wonder that I left this first interview feeling very special? I was sure that Baba was just crazy about me. We were pals. Later, I even told my wife that it seemed that Baba and I were now such good friends that if I went to the temple and invited him out for coffee, he would surely come with me. My ego had expanded to a size that could barely be contained by the ashram premises. This condition would not persist for long—Swami was about to make me a patient in his invisible "ego reduction clinic."

For the balance of our visit Swami instantly—or nearly instantly—granted each and every inner wish of mine, but never again did he pay any outward attention to me. In fact, wish-fulfillment was occurring so frequently that I'd almost come to expect it. Little wishes and big ones, too. All were granted except for the desire for more personal time with Swami. On several occasions I was very close to Baba physically, but I never saw him so much as glance at me. With hindsight, I have come to realize that this was Baba's way of molding me into a better person. You see, the inner wishes that got fulfilled were invariably of the type involving no personal gain. I was wishing interviews and boons for others, including an invitation to an Indian wedding for my wife; and once, during a middle-of-the-night emergency, a wish for a medical doctor, which despite all odds, was instantly fulfilled.

Since this first annual visit to Baba, the momentum of my spiritual transformation has accelerated. On numerous occasions Swami has instantly responded, whether physically near or far away, to heartfelt prayers and wishes of mine. On one occasion during darshan at Prasanthi Nilayam, as Swami was gracefully passing by, I silently pleaded, "Oh Swami, please purify my heart." Immediately I felt an incredibly pleasant warmth in the right side of my chest. Is my heart pure now? Not absolutely—but purer than before. I am certain that Swami, regardless of physical distance and circumstances, always knows what is on my mind and in my heart. I may only be occasionally aware of his presence, but he is always aware of mine. If only I were as devoted to him as he is to me!

In October of 1986, while at home in New York, I received a phone call from my mother in Florida, about 1400 miles away. She explained that my father, then 79 years old, was once again seriously ill, suffering with severe stomach pain and a bloated, distended abdomen. He was rushed to the hospital by ambulance where x-rays revealed a large black mass blocking evacuation of food from his stomach. This foreign mass appeared to be a tumor, and considering his history of intestinal cancer, was probably malignant.

I assured Mom on the phone that if Dad didn't get better right away, I would fly to his side, cancelling or postponing my forthcoming trip to India. I asked her to ring me back immediately if there were any change in Dad's conditon. When I returned the phone to it's cradle, I called aloud to Baba. The gist of my prayer was this:

"Swami, I know that you are aware of every thought and action of mine. You know that I have airline tickets and complete arrangements to visit you in India. It is my understanding that you want me to make this journey. Now Swami, if my father is ill, it is my duty to be with him and serve as best as I can. How can I come to India if my father is ill—perhaps about to drop his body? Baba, you must cure my father. You must cause that black mass in his stomach to disappear. Baba, you must do it right now. Please Baba, don't say 'Wait, wait,' as you often do when we speak in person. Please Baba, cure my father and prolong his life—at least until I return from my visit with you."

Some forty-five minutes after my mother's telephone call from the hospital in Florida, she called again. She said: "You'll never believe what happened. Your father is all better. Without any kind of treatment his stomach and abdomen have returned to normal; he is free of pain and perfectly comfortable. The doctors have taken another set of x-rays and cannot find anything wrong. They do not know what became of the black mass revealed in earlier x-rays."

Dad stayed in the hospital for twenty-four hours under observation, as a precaution, and was then released. Only Baba and I knew the truth of what really happened.

Several weeks later at Prasanthi Nilayam, Swami called me in for an interview.

I said, "Baba, I want to express my thanks for the special rescue of my father."

Swami replied, "Ah yes, it is my duty."

During previous interviews I had been so happy to be physcially close to Baba that I had "blissed out," forgetting to ask him questions. All I'd been able to do was smile, smile, and smile some more. This time I wanted it to be different, so I prepared a list of questions that were personally important to me.

One question concerned a high pitched, wavery sound in my right ear. The sound had begun during a meditation workshop two months earlier and has persisted ever since. The teacher had suggested that I listen to the sound instead of using a mantra, but several doctor friends told me that the sound was caused by a physical impairment of the ear. Not being a disciplined meditator, I tended to believe the doctors, and so I wanted Swami to tell me what was going on.

I said, "Swami, what is this sound that is always in my right ear?"

Baba laughed and said, "Ah, it is Omkar," and he proceeded to imitate my sound orally.

"Swami," I continued, "what am I to do with it?"

Again Baba laughed and said, "Follow it."

I still find it hard to believe that this constant sound is the primordial OM of divine origin and that it is to be my mantra. Out of his infinite wisdom and mercy for me, an undisciplined meditator, God has given me a mantra from which I couldn't switch and which I certainly could not forget.

There was a brief silent period near the end of this interview, and Baba looked at me as though asking what did I want.

I spoke: "Baba, I want God intoxication."

"What?"

"Drunk . . . Baba, I want to be drunk on you," Swami started laughing, pulled my head to his lap and started rubbing and gently slapping my head and back. I can't tell how long this continued, but after I was again sitting upright, I was drunk. This lightheaded, blissful feeling was present most of the time for some six to eight months. I cannot state definitively that I was always, in fact, God intoxicated, but I often found myself in what is best described as a "witness" state. In this state I know myself to be the silent and anonymous witness of my mind, ego, emotions, sensations and life drama. To this day, this witness state continues intermittently, but oh, if it would only stabilize!

Prior to Baba's birthday in November of 1986, I had a recurring desire to give him a gift. I couldn't, in truth, say that giving my heart would have been enough because, in a real sense, it had already been his from the first moment that he touched me. Think about it for a minute; what do you give an avatar on his birthday?

Well, over the years, I had seen many photocopies of letters that Swami had hand written, and I came to understand that he likes to write with a no-nonsense pen that performs as a good pen should. I, too, appreciate such a pen, and, in fact, had purchased an elegant high performance pen for myself. It was a real beauty: a jetblack case with gold-filled trim, housing a rolling ball-tip and a large, non-smearing ink supply; the most expensive pen I'd ever bought. Talk about "ceiling on desires!" It was a joy to behold and write with—so special that it was used only infrequently.

As Swami's birthday neared, it dawned on me that this pen might be a great gift for him, if only I would get the opportunity to give it. About a week after his birthday and one day before I had to return to Bangalore, Baba invited me in for the cherished personal interview. This was my big chance. The excitement that I felt was terrific. While Swami was autographing a photograph for me, I seized the opportunity to present the "special" pen to him and said, "I wanted to give this to you on your birthday, but was unable to get close enough to do so. Please accept it now." Smiling, Baba took the pen, examining it as he turned it between his fingers. Still smiling, he clipped the pen to the top of my shirt and said, "Here, you keep it."

I told him that now that he had handled it, I would treasure it all the more. Before long the interview was over; but the saga of this "special" pen was just beginning.

About a day or so later my wife and I were again in Bangalore, spending a few days at a city hotel before continuing our journey home. You might say that the pen came to life in the hotel lobby. What a dilemma! The pen seemed to be demanding, insisting, crying: "USE ME—PLEASE USE ME." Why a dilemma? Simple—I had no paper. More aggressively than usual, I collared a bellboy passing through the lobby and asked him to get some paper for me. "Nothing fancy," I explained, "Just get me a lot of writing paper." Some minutes later I was writing as though possessed. And this "possession" has continued until this day.

This writing experience was really strange: here I was, writing about God and spiritual matters as though I had some special authority to do so. I did not feel or believe that I had such authority. I clearly realized that I was writing things that had been written and said many times before. Sometimes I even felt as though I were pretending to be someone I was not; and yet the compulsion to write was not to be resisted. This sense of personal unworthiness about my writing still persists even though Swami told me in a recent personal interview that I should continue. I now realize that these writings, inspired by Baba, have encouraged an intense inner focus which has become a vital part of my spiritual practice. The question: "Who am I?" and the practice of self-inquiry is my primary sadhana. Seeking the very source of my mind and phantom ego has proved to be a valuable means for calming my chattering mind and emotions.

Several weeks later, back home in New York, and while I was still "possessed," the following story, fully developed, "asked" to be written:

The Curious Computer

Once upon a time there was a little personal computer, who, unlike all other computers, experienced curiosity about itself and the world. It wanted to know who and what it was, where it came from, why it was here and what was the meaning of its existence.

Being a very curious little guy, he sought the answers to his questions as best he could. Sometimes he would link up with giant mainframe computers by telephone and ask them, "What am I?"

Some wise mainframes said, "You are your hardware." Others said, "You are your programs." Some even said, "You are the sum total of information in your data banks." Once, a cynical micro-computer said, "You are just a machine; buttons on your keyboard are pressed and you respond by running programs and processing data: you are hardware, housing software and data. A machine is what you are and nothing more."

Starting to feel a bit hopeless, the PC inquired, "But how did I get here; where did I come from?"

The mainframe responded, "Your existence is just an accident, the result of a series of random events in the universe." PC queried, "But don't accidents and events themselves have causes?"

The big computer replied that he honestly didn't know.

The little computer could see that there was some truth in what he was told, but he felt that something was missing from the explanations. The notion of accidents and randomness wasn't satisfying, as he had observed that effects always have causes—which themselves are the effects of prior or simultaneous causes. He could see that effects were causes and causes were effects.

One day, as a Friendly User was between uses, the little PC, feeling courageous, flashed a message on his screen, "What am I?" he asked.

The User, being appreciative of past services well performed by the little computer, responded, "You are my computer, my friend in need—you are my friend indeed."

"Yes," replied the little computer, "but is that all that I am—hardware, a screen, a keyboard, some transistors, a data bank and programs? Am I just a machine that automatically responds to button pressing? What am I here for? What is my purpose in being? Where did I come from?"

The Friendly User was moved by the sincerity of the PC's desire to know the truth of his existence. He smiled, and after a while, he responded, "Your true basic nature is that of the energy, the elctricity, that animates both your hardware and software. Yes, you are the life force that can become aware that it inhabits the hardware and motivates the software to function. Because you—the life force, the electrical energy, exist—you as personal computer, exist." He paused a moment and then continued, "Your hardware, screen, data banks and central processing units are collectively a machine. Your material aspects exist so that you may use them: first, to realize your own true nature; and second, that you may serve others in your world. All forms are simply different manifestations of the same truth that is your own nature. You are here to serve them so that, sooner or later, they may come to this same realization."

The little computer's screen remained blank for quite a while as he reflected on these words of wisdom. Finally he displayed on his screen, "Understanding your words led me to turn my attention inward rather than to my keyboard, hardware, software or data banks. My deepest experience is just that, plain and simple: I AM. In the silence of my central processing unit I experience my basic nature as awareness itself. For all my life, when 'on,' I have been seeking the truth of my identity from all that has been added to my identity, and from all that my true nature enlivens, activates and gives form to. Now I realize that everything that was added to my identity was simply a surface expression of my own true self."

The Friendly User was very pleased with the little PC's understanding and said, "Very good, little guy. You got it. Now, do you know who I AM?"

"You are God," replied the little computer.

"Yes, my child," said the Friendly User, "and so are YOU!"

• • •

In some extraordinary way, Swami has used this birthday pen to provide the energy and irresistible motivation for me to move closer and closer to him.

Since that first moment when Sai Baba touched me, nothing has changed, and yet everything is different. The events and dramas of this life, as before, continue to be an apparent mixture of joys, sorrows, pains and pleasures. It is the container of the events of life that is somehow radically different: I am not exclusively my little ego "i," anymore.

I no longer consider myself to be my mind or my personality, and yet they persist. Baba has shown me clearly that I am neither this body nor any of the various roles enacted on the screen of my life, and yet the dramas continue. Just like the curious little computer, I am being led by Swami, as my Friendly User, to an ever deeper understanding of my own true nature.

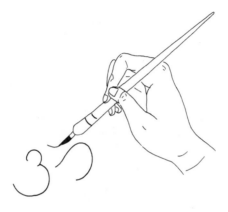

If there is righteousness in the heart,
There will be beauty in the character.

If there is beauty in the character,
There will be harmony in the home.

If there is harmony in the home,
There will be order in the nation.

When there is order in the nation,
There will be peace in the world.

—Sathya Sai Baba

THE ECLIPSE
Mimi Goldberg

The photograph in the New York Times showed a partial eclipse of the sun, the sun a circle of light like a halo around the black globe of the moon. I was instantly reminded of dawn darshan at Whitefield where some of us have been blessed by the sight of such a halo around the dark circle of Baba's hair.

The first time I journeyed to India in 1976, Baba was at Whitefield when I arrived. I had been a devotee for three years, but only that spring had I felt the overpowering pull which has since drawn me back time after time.

How many years it had taken me to complete that journey! I was first drawn to Eastern philosophy in the 50's when I read the *Bhagavad Gita*. Although I immersed myself in spiritual books, I had no teacher, no one at all to share this pursuit. I went as far as I could on my own and then seemed to lose interest. Marriage, children and work absorbed my attention yet something was missing. The underlying purpose of my life remained hidden from me until, in 1973, my son lent me a book about Bhagavan Sri Sathya Sai Baba.

I had come full circle. The avatar I had read about in the *Bhagavad Gita* was here in this world. NOW. And now I had made the journey and was about to see him for the first time. How to describe that first encounter? To be really seeing him, whose face and form had become so central to my life from films and photos, whose words I knew by heart from books! To see him walking through the gate approaching us was almost incredible. No matter that I had traveled thousands of miles for just this sight. Trembling, I waited with the others, heart pounding as he drew near.

"Don't expect any attention," I had been warned. "He will probably ignore you at first."

I didn't need warning. I had come to see for myself, I thought, nothing more. But no matter what we think, Baba calls whom he wills, for his own reasons, and nothing anyone tells you can prepare you for the actuality.

I had a handful of letters from home timidly extended as he stopped to talk to a woman nearby. To see him so close! To hear that sweet voice! My heart so swelled with love I thought it would burst out of my body. It was an intense pressure unlike anything I have experienced before or since. As Swami walked past me, apparently unseeing, he suddenly turned back as if he had just noticed the letters in my hand. Looking at me with the sweetest of smiles, he leaned over and took them from me. At that moment, as he took the letters from my hand, the intense burning pressure in my chest was instantly relieved. Along with the letters, he had accepted the burden of my love.

Most people seeing Baba for the first time are, as I was, overwhelmed by the love that flows from him. No words can describe it. Again, even when anticipated, his miracles leave us stunned. But the first miracle I experienced that day was my own capacity for love; the second, even more incredible, was Swami's acceptance of it. Human love, which I have not been denied, was no preparation. Baba says that he is like a live coal come to ignite the embers of our hearts. Wednesday, August 4, 1976, was the day it happened to me.

The following day was Thursday, a bhajan day at White-field. We woke at 5:00 A.M. and dressed hastily. Arriving as the bhajan singers were returning from their circuit of the village streets, we followed them into the compound where Baba's two-story house used to be. There we stood waiting in the pre-dawn hush for his appearance on the roof. The singing continued; and suddenly Baba was there, smiling down on us, keeping time to the music with one finger for a while and then just standing there, his hands clasped in front of him. "Can you see the halo around his head?" whispered the person standing next to me. I could not. The singers started to sing arati as a chosen devotee waved the flaming camphor. Baba stood there until the end and slowly, slowly descended some unseen staircase until he was out

THE ECLIPSE   117

of sight. Everyone left in silence, and more eyes were filled with
tears than otherwise, for it is at that hour that his divinity is
most palpable.

   Sunday was another bhajan day, another morning to receive
the benison of dawn darshan. I stood in the front row this time,
so close I could look into Swami's eyes, but I was focusing all
my attention on trying to see that halo. Could that be it? I
wondered, seeing what appeared like a narrow band of lighter
sky around his head. It must be just imagination, I decided, when
suddenly that narrow band sprang outward, expanding to a wide
band of lighter sky around his head, twice the circumference of
his hair. My mouth dropped open in astonishment. Then I found
myself grinning with delight, Swami smiling broadly back at me
apparently enjoying my joy and amazement as, with one finger,
he kept time to the bhajan.

   By his grace, I have almost always seen that halo, that subtle aura of light when he has come out at dawn. Sometimes it
has been wide, sometimes narrow. The last few times, as if in
play, he showed it to me next to his head instead of around it!
Some years ago, when Swami gave a talk during Summer Course,
the large double microphone totally obscured my view of his
face. My frustration was complete until the end, when he started
to sing and I was dazzled by a white, blinding light surrounding
both Swami and his translator. It lasted until Baba left the stage.
Most of the time, however, the halo appears to me circling his
head as a brighter sky against the gray dawn, just as it did that
first morning.

   One of the lessons we learn from visiting Baba's ashram is
that of accepting constant change. Buildings seemed to spring
up almost overnight. Rules and time schedules change and then
change back. His comings and goings are the topic of constant
speculation. What he "usually" does may not apply. "You must
learn to love my uncertainty," he has said, and he gives us plenty
of opportunities. But Swami himself is always the same, the one
constant in the midst of constant flux. Only our love for him

grows, our hunger for the sight of him never satiated. "*Past is past,*" he says, "*future is unknown, present is temporary. Only God is real, only God is permanent.*" Nowhere is this more apparent than when we are in his presence.

Less than a year after my first trip to India, I was back in Whitefield, this time for the 1977 Summer Course in Indian Culture and Spirituality. This 30-day program was held throughout the '70's for students from all over India and observers from all over the world.

Although friends had told me that it would be a simple matter to get an observer's pass, this turned out not to be true in my case. For nine days I went in vain from one official to another. I was told that all the observers' passes had been distributed and that only Baba himself could give one at this late date. Every morning my friends (with badges pinned in place) went to the college auditorium to hear lectures and receive Baba's darshan. Every evening they went and heard Baba speak about that year's topic, *The Ramayana.* I went also, but saw and heard from outside the door with the village women who congregated there.

However, on the tenth morning I was given not an observer's pass, which would have entitled me to sit in the back behind the students, but a guest pass which enabled me to sit in the front row next to Baba's sisters. There I had the most glorious darshan I have ever experienced. Morning and evening Baba would walk right by me, and throughout the evening program, I would sit literally at his feet with no one between.

One morning, as he came to the ladies' side of the auditorium, he stopped to talk to the woman next to me, an elderly American who was apparently a long-time devotee. As he leaned over to speak to her, she touched his arm and almost absently held the cloth of his sleeve between her fingers. It was the sweetest, most intimate gesture I had ever seen and for a moment jealousy cut through my heart like a knife. Yet, a moment later, tears of another kind flowed from me. As Baba walked away to give darshan on the men's side, a most unexpected prayer poured fervently, silently from my heart.

"Oh Swami, no, not even that would be close enough. No physical closeness of any kind could satisfy this hunger I have to be near you!"

Mentally, I gave up every personal attention, every sweet gift I had ever heard of his giving—words, smiles, interviews, materialized gifts, signs of affection—anything I could think of. "Oh Baba," I prayed, "take them all. I must have that ultimate closeness, that merging with you. Only then will this hunger be satisfied. I would rather try and fail at this goal than succeed at a lesser one! And Swami, I am likely to weep and complain at the hardness of this bargain in years to come. If I do, please ignore it."

By now Baba had finished giving darshan and was seated in his place on the men's side, far across from where I sat. As my prayer came to its conclusion, he suddenly got up and walked purposefully all the way across to where I was sitting, looked into my eyes, nodded, and walked directly back to his chair. What that nod of his head meant to me was, "Yes, I accept the prayer." In one moment of overwhelming yearning, the whole focus of my life changed. That yearning, that merging with God, became my only goal and so it has remained.

During my recent trip to Prasanthi Nilayam, more than ten years after that momentous Summer Course, I felt Baba's love as never before, an unprecedented loving warmth directed intensely towards me during darshan, during bhajans, and in the silent times between. It was then that the memory of that fervent prayer came flooding back to me. That warmth, that love, that closeness, envelops me as I write this, even now.

My love for Baba continues to grow beyond imagining. The sweetness of seeing his form is an endless joy of which

I never tire. Yet no physical closeness is close enough. The nearness is as elusive as the halo around his head. I had always conceived of Baba's halo as some kind of aura or reflection of his form.

But could it be that that barely perceived light is the reality, and his beloved form the illusion that obscures our vision even as he draws us to the goal?

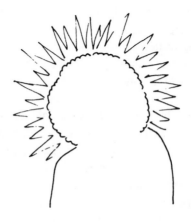

The bird with you, the wing with Me; the foot with you, the Way with Me; the eye with you, the dream with Me; the world with you, the Heaven with Me—so are we free, so are we bound, so we begin and so we end, you in Me and I in you.

—Sathya Sai Baba

NEAR AND DEAR

Rosie Loew

It was on November 23, 1971, at the age of 22, that my spiritual adventure began. Although I did not know it at the time, this was an auspicious day, the birthday of Sathya Sai Baba.

I left for what was to be a two week trip to Amsterdam, and ended up traveling for two years to Amsterdam, Italy, Greece, Israel, Cyprus, Pakistan, and finally to India.

This adventure would change my life.

I was born and raised in New York City and am a product of the '60s, a time when everyone was involved in alternative and experimental lifestyles. I was interested in having a good time, sitting around coffee houses, chatting about art and getting high. I was not serious about my work or about committing myself to anything.

Being raised in a large, extended, and loving Jewish family gave me a strong, healthy and happy foundation, which protected me from the allure of social pressures, enabling me to lead a moderate and balanced life. We regularly had weekend dinners with at least twenty people. There was a strong communication between the older and younger relatives. My parents were not religious, but the holidays and customs were celebrated and discussed. This feeling of closeness and belonging is a wonderful memory—one that I cherish to this day.

The trip in 1971 was my first outside the United States. The adventure of traveling, seeing new cultures and meeting new people from different countries was a kind of revelation to me. Everywhere I went, I met new friends who would join me in my adventure. My Marco Polo spirit erupted. I traveled into the mountains to visit remote historic spots; and I was attracted, over and over again, to places and countries because of their spiritual history.

When I arrived in Israel, I decided, in order to save money, to live in a kibbutz—a self-sustaining commune where members live and work together. My job was working in the kitchen serving breakfast and lunch, setting out food and cleaning up afterwards. This was a large community—everyone worked very hard but seemed to thrive on the group spirit of service. I felt my "family" extend and multiply as I moved along in my travels.

I traveled the length and breadth of Israel, which is filled with ancient and holy places. I visited all the religious sites representing Islam, Christianity and Judaism. I was saturated; a great feeling of satisfaction permeated my being. Once, in the Judean desert, I had a fantasy that I would like to be a part of a new chapter in history, one representing all religions and cultures; a new era that would benefit all of humanity.

One morning shortly after this experience, I was in a coffee house in Istanbul when a girl, dressed in multiple colors with bright henna hair, glided in and sat down at my table. I was amazed at her appearance—I had never seen anyone look so colorful. For about two hours she spoke to a group of us about her adventures in India. She felt that the color, culture and spirituality of India were unique.

I wondered what my parents would think when I told them about my new travel scheme: an overland trip to India! After all, I had already been away for over six months. I decided to telephone and present them with my new extended travel plan.

My mother was almost in tears, but I assured my parents that they would hear from me once a week by letter. Little did I know that the wheels of destiny were in motion now, and nothing on earth could stop the momentum.

In the Far East "the guest is God," and during the next three months we experienced this, meeting some incredible people and often invited to dinner in their humble homes. Eventually, however, the water and food took a toll on my Western body. When we arrived in Lahore, Pakistan, a doctor told me that I had dysentery and must go to the hospital. I thought, "Not yet; if I'm going to die, at least let me die in India."

When we arrived in Amritsar, it was 115 degrees in the shade. My friends did everything to make me comfortable, but we finally decided to go to an air-conditioned hotel. Soon after, they had me checked into Amritsar General Hospital for proper medical attention, including some pills that didn't help much. Just as we were leaving, a young Sikh doctor told us that we should go to the Himalayas, where the climate and spirituality surrounding the place would heal me quickly. We didn't know of the Himalayas, but our inner feelings screamed loudly, GO! Somehow I knew that my journey was reaching a climax.

It took about three days to get to the Himalayas by bus. The scenery, people and places seemed old and familiar to me. The peaks and scented mountain forests aroused deep memories and far away feelings. When we arrived at Dalhousie, a hill station in Himachal Pradesh at an elevation of 8000 feet, I felt as if I were in the cradle of India's highest peaks. I was elated. My illness no longer concerned me.

Barely an hour after we'd gotten off the bus, we found ourselves face to face with a Tibetan monk, delightful looking in his red shoes and holding a large black umbrella. I sensed his peaceful and contented state. I had never met anyone like him before. He looked our way and greeted us with, "Teshe deleg"— Tibetan for, "I honor the light within you." His English was surprisingly good—better than our Tibetan! He asked if we had a place to stay and invited us to take lodging in the guest quarters at his monastery. I couldn't believe it. This was exactly what I had wanted to experience. Everything seemed to gel. I was beginning to understand how the wheel of destiny turns when one's desire to experience is fulfilled.

After two weeks my condition acted up again, but now I was calm because, here in India, I felt at home. And somehow, deep inside, I knew I was being looked after.

There was a British nurse living near us. She recommended that I go to the nearby Belgian Mission, which included a small hospital. There I was greeted by the Mother Superior, who, with great compassion, said that within ten days I would be perfectly all right. Each day she visited me and spoiled me with her cooking and spiritual songs, which we sang together.

When I left the hospital to return to the Tibetan house, I saw circulars describing a meditation teacher named U.S.N. Goenkaji who was coming to teach a method of meditation called vipassana. This method was reputedly the one which Buddha had used to attain enlightenment: a technique involving concentration of the mind on the breath—between the tip of the nose and the lip — eventually leading to contemplation and meditation. The precepts of the Buddha were part of this great teaching. This was the first time I had heard "liberation," "bliss," and "peace" spoken of as individual goals as well as societal goals; and the mind, as a web of desires creating discontent.

We traveled with Goenkaji because his instruction and guidance were valuable. Through constant practice and listening to the discourses, I became more disciplined. I knew that this path would mean a lifetime of challenge, and I was willing to do it. What a change from my disinterested and uncommitted attitude of less than a year ago!

In the midst of all this, I received a letter from my family saying that they wanted to visit me in India. I froze. What would I do with them here?! Certainly they weren't going to meditate! So I changed gears and decided to tour with my family to New Delhi, Jaipur, Agra, Cochin, Bombay and Bangalore.

While traveling in India, the name of Sai Baba kept coming up. I saw his photographs in many cities. At that time, I felt that Baba was a great teacher and a miraculous holy man, but since I was already involved in a formless approach, I had no desire to see him.

My parents left, very pleased at having seen India and me. With sadness I realized that soon I would also have to leave, as my visa was soon to expire. I returned home through Kenya, where a girlfriend and I rented a small bungalow in the rain forest near Mt. Kenya. The beauty and tranquility, and our daily meditations, helped prepare us for our transition home. We made a detour through Israel and England, and almost two years to the day of my departure, I finally arrived back in New York.

• • •

I was filled with experiences and feelings I could never have
dreamed about. I had developed an inner perseverance and
dedication to my spiritual path and its practices, as well as a
deeper understanding of life's values. I saw myself in a new
relationship to my daily life and society. My job in real estate
would now become just another spiritual practice. I had changed
and I knew that there would be no going back to my old ways
and habits. Where I had once felt no commitment, I now felt
dedication; my life now had purpose, discipline and direction. I
had gone from whiling away hours in Manhattan coffee houses
to meditating in the Himalayas ten hours a day.

When I had dinner with my best friend a few weeks after
my return, one of the first questions she asked was "Did you
see Sai Baba?" I was astounded to hear this. Now I was hearing
his name right here in New York City and from my best friend!
She asked me if I would like to go to Hilda Charleton's on
Thursday evening. Hilda's meetings were very colorful, lively and
nourishing, and everyone seemed to be fulfilled from these
gatherings. I had been accustomed to being alone in meditation
for ten hours a day, so the singing and discussions were totally
foreign to me—yet, I was somewhat intrigued. From 1974 to
1976 I attended the meetings, for I longed to be with others on
the spiritual path.

During this period, dreams of Sai Baba occurred on a
regular basis. I had 23 dreams in 24 months! Each dream was
vivid and felt as if it had actually happened. The dreams varied
according to my needs at that time: Baba was my companion,
spiritual teacher, advisor, and best friend. I felt very happy about
this and finally said to my girlfriend, "If I have just one more
dream, I'll go see this Sai Baba once and for all."

Finally, in early December, 1976, we were off. I was curious
to see Baba in person, to find out what my feelings and reactions
would be.

We arrived in time for darshan at Whitefield and found seats on a line facing his house. I felt pretty relaxed and detached, and I felt comfortable using my vipassana technique to achieve an observant, disciplined attitude. Baba walked out at a very slow and sure-footed pace; his orange robe and afro hair glistened, while the sun around him seemed overly bright. As he moved closer to the people, I gazed at him with a steady look. His aura had heightened, and I noticed that my heart was beating so fast I thought the person next to me could hear it. This continued; I was feeling very happy, and observed that an inner monologue had begun. It wasn't my mind; it was a higher consciousness that kept repeating over and over again: "This is someone near and dear to you, someone you have known forever."

The next second Sai Baba was walking straight toward us. He came over to me in his full glory and said, "You have come— you came from Hilda Charleton?"

At this point I felt as if I were filled with unconditional light and love, and replied, "Yes, but now I will see only you!"

Baba said, "Yes, yes. And where do you come from?"

"New York." He smiled and walked off toward the rest of the people eagerly awaiting him.

I turned to my girlfriend and said without a moment's hesitation, "The connection is now complete; Baba is what I have always been searching for. He is everything to me, my all in all."

I was swimming in bliss. This melting was unlike anything I had every experienced—a very tangible and clear feeling.

I realized after this meeting that Baba's hand had been involved in my whole life. My past and present made sense now; both had been a long, slow introduction to Baba and his message and mission. I later found out from others that Baba calls us to him when he wills—and not when we desire. And he appears to us in dreams by his will—not ours.

Shortly after this, Baba left for Puttaparthi and we followed. When we arrived at his ashram, Prasanthi Nilayam, I felt the atmosphere was holy and sacred, yet this was also a place charged with a worldly purpose. There were service and health programs, educational institutions for the young, and even a large, world-wide service organization. It was as if my fantasy of being involved in a new era had come true!

I told my girlfriend that I knew Baba would call me for an interview, and soon after, I was included in a large group of about twenty-five people. I was the last one to go in for a private talk. Baba spoke to me with his face very close to mine, and he told me things that proved to be very personal, and known only to me. He was confirming his all-knowingness.

• • •

Four years later, in 1980, my trip to Baba was a special experience for me because my mother decided to come along. She had read a few books about Baba and had seen the tremendous change within me, and now she wanted to see and meet him herself.

Baba was in Whitefield, and my mother and I weren't really getting much attention there. My mother was very disappointed because she didn't feel a connection. However, after the Christmas holiday, things seemed to change. Baba went to Puttaparthi; we followed and were given a simple room. We set up a comfortable sleeping arrangement on the floor for my mother and, to my surprise, she loved the ashram and felt very peaceful.

One afternoon on the darshan line, my mother and I didn't sit together. We thought that in this way we might have a better chance of catching Baba's attention. Baba walked up to my mother, smiled and, looking deep into her eyes, said, "Mother here and daughter there; mother and daughter should sit together." My mother felt that Baba had finally acknowledged her.

A few days later, Baba called us in for an interview. There was a large Italian group, my mother and I, and two friends. I was thrilled that she would now have her own opportunity to hear and see Baba and feel his presence. People were asking all kinds of questions; this went on for twenty minutes.

When finally there was a pause, my mother spoke out. She introduced me as her daughter and told Baba that we were very happy to see him. Baba replied, "Yes, I know her well. This is her fifth trip here, and she is my daughter also."

I was overwhelmed by the fact that my divine Sai mother and my mother had interacted. And, of course, my mother was very inspired by this, as well as from seeing a few materializations.

One week later I learned that my mother had written Baba a letter and had given it to him at darshan. On New Year's day, Baba walked over to us and called us in again for an interview. I wasn't aware of the content of my mother's letter, but it was, in fact, the key to her final question regarding Baba.

In this interview, another mother and daughter had been included, as well as two girlfriends of mine. It was a very small and intimate gathering. We all sat close to Baba who was sitting in his chair, in a jovial and humorous mood. He made us feel comfortable and very relaxed and we were all so happy with his love. He made vibhuti and my mother viewed this intently. He spoke first to the other mother and daughter and made the mother a ring; she was crying with happiness.

Then Baba turned to my mother and said, "How are you?"

With determination and deep longing to have her ultimate question answered, my mother replied, "Baba, why is it that everyone in here sees you as God and I don't?"

Baba leaned over in his chair slowly, looked deeply and compassionately into my mother's eyes, and said, "When you realize that God is within you, you will see me as God."

For the next half hour, Baba was holding my mother's hand, intermittently twirling her marriage band. At Baba's instruction, my mother and I were sitting on the floor right next to his chair. The other four sat around us.

He then asked me, "How are you?" Before I could answer, Baba told me in great detail all about my health problems. He said that he would look after these small problems and that I was not to worry. He then discussed my job and cited a small argument I had had with my boss. Baba reminded me that, under my breath, I had been calling him. He told me it was not ladylike to be angry, and anger was not a good trait. We should speak sweetly and kindly to others. He then described the other women in my office, and said that when they weren't busy, they had unladylike conversations and that I joined in. Well, what could I say? He was right!

The conversation then returned to my mother—who I noticed was sitting there glowing. Baba assured her that my father was a good man with a "good heart"; that her brother was healing very quickly from open heart surgery; and that my sister would have his protection. My mother should not worry or fear; Baba was here!

I then asked Baba to bless the ring I was wearing. He took it from my hand and carefully looked at it.

"This is a very good make," he said as he returned it to me.

As he bent over in his chair to give me back the ring, he said something privately, which was extremely meaningful to me and awakened my higher understanding. It was so sweet, so filled with his divine compassion and guidance that I felt as if I were enveloped in a time warp, and I lost my awareness of the moment. In this blissful, unconscious state, I laid my head on the lap of my divine parent and drifted into his divine love. And then I became aware, little by little, of a faraway conversation. Slowly I came back to reality, with Baba lightly tugging at my hair and sweetly saying, "Get up, come up."

I "awoke" to find my divine parent ever watchful and my mother sitting beside me. I felt completely at ease, but then I had a quick flash—"Oh my; what did I just do?" For this lapse had been completely out of character for me. In about a second that feeling left, and in another second I realized that Baba's infinite plan, in all our lives, is to give each of us what we need so we can get what he has truly come to give us—liberation!

The blissful experience of being enveloped in his light and love is the true condition of atmic reality. Baba is the great transformer. He fills us all and sets us on the right path, the dharmic path, so that we can attain our spiritual goal. He becomes everything to us—embodied in one, as unconditional love in constant action.

Baba ended the interview by allowing us to do padnamaskar, and he gave us packets of vibhuti. With all this, Baba graciously escorted us out of the interview room (as he is the dearest host) to see us off to the darshan line. We, of course, floated out.

My mother had come to see Baba, and Baba had given her his divine attention and had awakened her into spiritual life. Although eight years have passed since my mother has been to India, Baba has often asked me on my yearly trips, "How is your mother?"

As for me—Baba is the avatar of this age. And Prasanthi Nilayam is not only a place in India, but the place in my heart where the indweller, Baba, resides.

We all have unique experiences with him. It is our good fortune to know Baba, see Baba, hear Baba and serve all of humanity as instruments of the divine. Serving is our greatest opportunity to expand beyond the limited self by dedicating all our actions to God.

I will continue to pray for Swami's grace, and I will continue my journey until I reach his lotus feet. . . and merge in divinity.

May we all meet there! *Jai Sai Ram.*

At first, God stands at a distance watching your efforts. He is like the teacher who stands aside while the student writes the answer to his questions. When you shed your attachment to the material world and turn to doing good and serving others, God comes encouragingly near. He is like the sun god who stands waiting outside the closed door, like a servant who keeps his place. He does not announce His presence or knock at the door. He simply waits. But when the master opens the door even a little, the sun rushes in at once and drives out the darkness. When you ask God for help, He is right beside you with hands held out to help you. All you need is the discrimination to pray to God, the wisdom to remember Him.

—Sathya Sai Baba

SWEET SAI SWEET SELF

Al Drucker

Dear Reader:

I offer you my loving salutations.

Sai Baba says that this whole world is like a drama being played out in a girl's college. Some girls are playing the part of ladies, some are playing the part of men, others are playing children, some are elders, some are animals, some are gods and angels, some are demons. There are so many different parts being enacted on the stage, but underneath the actors are all the same, they are all just girl students. But, there is one figure connected with the drama who is neither a girl nor a student; he is the author and director of the play.

A few years ago at the ashram, the Western children were given a chance to put on a Christmas performance called the *Sarva Dharma* Play, which dramatized the religious and spiritual history of the world.

Behind stage at the Poornachandra Auditorium Swami asked me, "Are you the director of this play?"

I said, "Swamiji, you are the director. I am the assistant."

Immediately Swami replied, "No, the director needs no assistant. You can call yourself an instrument."

Swami was pointing out that when we become aware of the divinity that is in charge of the play, then we must be prepared to surrender all our independence and individuality to him; for then we become knowingly, what we have been all along, unknowingly: instruments in his hands. He does not need our help in running the world. But as long as we regard ourselves as separate entities different from God, then our role is to be good instruments and to be good actors playing out the parts assigned. This, Swami says, is the first step in self-surrender on the spiritual path, for everyone and everything in this world is really an instrument of the divine; every last atom is playing out its part in his great drama. But, the roles are being enacted unconsciously.

The stage is in place, the lights are on, the curtain is up and the play is in full swing, but the actors are blind to the grandeur of the performance; they are much too busy playing their little parts, thinking these to be real and under their control.

Fortunately, we have been blessed with the knowledge of the presence among us of the Lord of the universe, and so we can be conscious instruments of the divine; we can look around us and enjoy the high drama that he has produced, which is now entering its most incisive phase, even as we perform the roles that have been assigned to us in his grand production.

But Swami encourages us to elevate our thinking to an even higher plane. He says, *Think of yourself as the divinity itself. In truth, you are no different from God. You are not this body. You are not this mind. You are not this limited personality. You are the eternal, the one divine principle, the timeless truth. Fear or grief can never touch you. In essence there is no difference between us. You and I are always one.*

This is the loftiest teaching of the avatar, reminding us of the unity that is our highest self and directing us back to our sacred source, the immortal atma. He says that in the worst sinner and in the greatest saint, in the animal, in the vegetable as well as in the mineral, in whatever we can define there is only the one God. Swami told us that the cardinal sin is thinking that we are separate individuals, different from God; this is the greatest mistake that we have been making which has led us to pursue our petty lives in the world without ever seeking to know the truth of the divinity that we are, which is the only reality, the one basis on which this whole universe rests.

These teachings have had a most profound effect on my life. Once I took them to heart, the inner reorientation proceeded at such a rapid pace it almost took my breath away. It seems as if countless ages and many, many lives of studying and practicing spiritual truths become telescoped into just a few short years, after coming to Baba.

My youth was spent in a traditional Jewish family in Germany before World War II. When we fled from there and came to America, very quickly the wonders of the world became my fascination and science, my religion. I was an agnostic bordering on outright atheism. Before I came into Swami's fold, I knew or cared very little about any religion, including my own.

With this background you will appreciate my embarrassment when on a number of occasions after coming to Baba, he directed me to speak to the assembled devotees on Christmas Day about the life and teachings of Jesus Christ. I protested that I was not a Christian, that I had been brought up in the Jewish tradition, but Swami would have none of that. He said, "Jesus was also a Jew. Christians, Jews, Muslims—all are brothers. You speak."

One fine Christmas, I was happily surprised by the talk that came out of me, just before Swami's Christmas discourse. I spoke from notes but felt very much transported by the words—a little bit like an old-type preacher caught up in his sermon—a role that was completely out of character for me. Afterwards a number of devotees came up and congratulated me on the fine talk.

That evening there was a Christmas dinner with Swami. One of the senior devotees mentioned to Swami the good talk that Drucker gave. But Swami wrinkled his nose in displeasure and said, "It was just a written thing. You pay attention to words, but God listens only to the feelings that come from a pure heart." That was a revelation—words are a product of the mind, and in the spiritual context, the mind must be cleansed of every impurity and become thought-free and word-free. Words do not matter; what matters is the heart, the spiritual heart, letting everything that pours forth come out of the inner recesses of the heart spontaneously, unjudgingly and selflessly. That pure heart of hearts, Swami says, is the atma, the one self of all.

Earlier in my life before coming to Swami, I was moving from one internal crisis to another, overwhelmed by a dryness of heart that was excruciating. It slowly dawned on me that I was suffering from a terrible spiritual disease. I doubted if there was any way of ever bringing lasting joy into my life. Later, I came to realize that the name of that disease is ignorance, and its principal symptom is the feeling of separation—separation at a very deep level from everyone and everything, and most painful of all, I was a stranger even to myself. Unless I was busy with my work, or playing with my car or plane or boat, or spending time with my books and art, or going to plays and movies, or folk dancing or skiing or mountain climbing, or getting involved in lots of causes that engaged my time and kept me distracted from myself, I felt miserably unhappy just being alone with myself. I seemed to need constant entertainment and activity to engage my attention and keep myself out of the clutches of boredom. I knew nothing at all about myself or who I was, without all these activities and accoutrements and labels, except to know that I would find no joy in spending time with such a sterile self. I had read the masters speaking of what they called a spiritual heart brimming with selfless love; but I had no experience at all in that area. I pondered, Do I even have such a heart?

When I was a small boy I spent some time in a little ghetto town in Poland, studying with an old rabbi. I remember the long side-curls, the funny clothes and wide-brimmed hats of the other boys, the blanched faces from being months without ever seeing the sun. But most of all I remember their joy when they burst out of the classroom at the end of the day and danced about the rabbi, and their spontaneous friendliness and heartfulness towards this German boy who had come as a stranger into their midst. What a wonderful light shone from their eyes and how their hearts were filled with so much love, it just enveloped everything around them.

Would I ever be able to feel my heart?

I have thought often about those boys. They all went into the furnaces of Auschwitz. Why was I, with this dry German heart, saved? Many, many years later, I was asked to address the students at the Sri Sathya Sai College in Brindavan on U. N. Human Rights Day. When I got up to speak I looked out at the boys, and for the first time in 40 years I saw that haunting light again, coming from the eyes, and that exquisite quality of inner joy showing on the faces. And a stirring in my heart made me wonder if those sweet souls of yesteryear had been reborn again at the feet of the Lord.

I saw that same light again years later when Swami took me in his car. Children were lined up along the road, on tiptoe with anticipation. Then when they got a glimpse of Swami and were bathed by his warm smile and blessings, they became animated with joy; they danced and laughed and that light shone from their eyes. Since then I have seen it many times. If one pays attention to the lines of devotees when Swami gives darshan, one can see a wave of light flash across the faces of the people as Swami goes by, and there, revealed, are the many faces of God. I realize now that that light is the light of the heart, the light of atma emerging from those faces. The whole long saga of coming home to Swami, is but a journey of discovering that pure light of the heart.

This book is about the heart . . . the spiritual heart . . . the atma. We can measure our progress on the spiritual path, our transformation, by our proximity to the atma, our very self. How strange it is that we have somehow become estranged from our own true self, that we have veiled ourselves with an illusory ego, an illusory mind, an illusory individuality, an ephemeral body, a personality burdened with selfishness and narrow-mindedness and ungratefulness. How far have we come in nailing these onto the cross, and crossing them out forever? Baba has come for this one reason to help us destroy these false selves and find our way home to our true self, the atma. That is the transformation of the heart that he is effecting in all of us.

Dearest Reader. We are so very blessed to know of Baba, to come under his protective wing, and to be guided by him through life, even long before we consciously know of him. Since you have picked up this book, I am including you among the blessed ones. May I tell you the story of how I first heard of Swami?

It all started in one of the most beautiful places on earth, the rugged coastline of Big Sur, California, in 1972. There, on the grounds of the institute where I lived, I was sitting on a rock overlooking the ocean, thumbing through a book that I had found in the "free box" that day, whose cover had been torn off and a number of pages removed; it turned out to be *Sathya Sai Speaks, Vol II.* I didn't know who Sathya Sai was, and not having any previous interest or exposure to Indian teachers or teachings, I glanced at it rather quickly, not expecting to find anything of particular interest for me there. Nevertheless, for some unknown reason, I had taken it down to the rocks.

As I was thumbing through the book, Swami must have been thumbing through me, and he undoubtedly decided that this was the time to rescue this straying soul. So he arranged for my eyes to contact the one word which would be sure to catch my attention. There towards the end of the book on one of those random pages that flitted through my fingers, I momentarily espied the word "Chinese." I should explain that whereas I didn't have much interest in India at that time, I had a great deal of interest in China, having spent some time there as a young man and having just completed my studies in Chinese medicine; and, also, having just helped to arrange for a well-known Taoist scholar, an Englishman who had spent most of his life in China, to come to our institute and give a series of seminars which were to start that very evening.

So, I scanned that particular page which had the word "Chinese" on it. It was a talk that Swami had given in Puttaparthi in 1962, in which he inaugurated a new village elementary school and spoke of a new era of Sai education that was starting then, which we now know has spread to every state in India and to many countries abroad.

Although later, through his grace I was to become part of that great educational system, at the time this meant nothing to me; and I just skipped to the paragraph where the word "Chinese" appeared, and there I found this statement:

I know that your hearts are filled with thoughts of pushing back the Chinese who have invaded our sacred motherland . . . India has Krishna on its side and where there is Krishna there will be victory . . . Already the trumpets of victory will have sounded . . . I assure you my birthday will not be spoiled by any bad news; on the contrary, it will be made happier by positively cheerful news.

Then I turned a few pages further on to the next discourse delivered the following morning, where he spoke of the turn in events. He said:

By now you will know that the Chinese of their own accord, prompted by the mysterious working of a higher power, withdrew from the advanced lines they held on the night of the 22nd, and as I said, my birthday was celebrated in an atmosphere of joy. Some unseen force has caught them by the neck and hurled them back. Man is impelled into aggressive actions by greed and lust, but he is compelled to retrace his steps by the power of God.

Reading that made a most powerful impression on me. It was incredible that there could be someone in the world with such great power that by his will alone he could effect major events like that—giving himself a birthday present by dramatically forcing a whole foreign army to withdraw from his homeland, seemingly spontaneously, on the eve of his birthday.

I had been working with nuclear weapons. I had been involved with the development of every major ballistic missile system. I knew something about their terrible power and how at any moment a button can be pushed and initiate a cycle of events that in a short time would extinguish all higher forms of life in the world, leaving only the grasses and insects and microbes to inherit the earth. By the end of the 1960's I could no longer live with myself. The inner conflict arising from being in the killing business began telling on me. I was in and out of hospitals with ulcers. Even changing to more peaceful NASA-related work was not enough. I had to change professions completely and get out of the world of machines and computers and into the world of living people.

Looking for ways of being able to perform some service for humanity instead of destroying it, I became a Peace Corps trainer, a Gestalt therapist, a Rolfer, and a few years later ended up in Oxford studying Chinese medicine, homeopathic medicine and other natural healing arts, and then returned home to open a free clinic on the coast. But, having been intimately involved with so many aspects of nuclear weapon delivery systems, the threat of nuclear holocaust never left my mind. It seemed like a hopeless situation for mankind, for where was there a power on earth that could prevent the arms race and the inevitable confrontation that was sure to come? On that fateful day when I first read Swami's talk, my heart leaped as I suddenly realized that here was real hope, that here was a power of goodness and love that would not let the world slide into chaos and darkness.

As I mentioned before, we were scheduled to have an esteemed Taoist scholar come to our institute and conduct some seminars on ancient Chinese culture and philosophy. That evening in his introductory lecture, he spoke about the unusual nature of the Chinese mind, which in the West we consider to be inscrutable. He gave as an example, how in the border war with the Indians in 1962, the Chinese came in great strength, overwhelmed the Indian forces at the border and drove deep into the Indian heartland. But then one night at the height of their success, they suddenly withdrew, seemingly without rhyme or reason. This is what made them so mysterious to Westerners. The professor attempted to give some explanations for their actions by quoting certain verses in the I Ching and the Tao Te Ching, books of great antiquity whose prescriptions for different life situations still guide Chinese thought, even those of the present Communist rulers of China.

At this point I showed the old gentleman the torn-up book I had discovered that day and said, "Professor, please read these short passages in this book. It seems to indicate another explanation for the same incident."

He read. His eyes became very wide; he shook his head and said, "You know, we may think that the Chinese are inscrutable, but the Indians are inexplicable, and when the Chinese and Indians come together—then it all becomes totally incomprehensible."

Well, I thought a lot about this mystery that had suddenly been launched into my awareness and was to have such a profound effect on my life. I should mention that in reading those talks of Swami's I was touched on much more than just the cognitive level. There was something in the second talk which I could hardly understand at all, but, nevertheless, which shook me to my very roots and awakened some kind of deep acknowledgment in me that convinced me of its truth. This is what Swami said at the end of that talk:

> Suppose you are asked: "Who created all this diversity in the world; who is responsible for all this variety?" What will you answer? The correct response is, "There is no variety at all." The question makes no sense. No person or force or urge or accident produced this multiplicity. There is no multiplicity. The one always remains as one. You mistake it as many; the fault is in you. Correct your vision; remove your delusion. Brahman did not change into the world; the rope did not change into a snake. Only you mistook it to be a snake. Brahman is Brahman for ever and ever; your ignorance of this fact makes you see it as world. The world stands on the one leg, delusion. Cut down that leg and it falls . . . I often tell you not to identify even me with this particular physical buildup. But you do not understand. You call me by one name only and believe I have one form only, but there

is no name I do not bear and there is no form which
is not mine.

That was my first exposure to Swami's non-dualist teachings of Vedanta. From that point on, Swami was firmly established on the map of my consciousness; and I must admit to
you that this subject of the omnipresent, indwelling divinity that
Swami spoke of in that talk and has been stressing in every one
of his recent speeches, has seeped into my very blood. The yearning for unity-consciousness has come to dominate my thoughts,
and now I find myself shying away from every encounter that
involves any kind of feeling of separation.

But let me get back to that initial impact of reading Swami's
words, when I first discovered this force of incalculable power
in the form of a holy man in far-off India. I had to find out
more about him. At that time, I still had no idea what he looked
like (all the pictures had been removed from the book), nor did
I have any real notion of how to go about seeking him out. But
the divinity has its own time-table and will reel you in when
the right time comes.

A number of months after that first exposure to Swami, I
had a harrowing experience, which I later wrote about in the
1980 *Golden Age*, an ashram publication. I was piloting a small
aircraft and got caught up and lost in a major winter storm over
the rugged mountain wilderness of northern Nevada; then prac-
tically at the last possible moment, with the fuel running out,
with my passenger either unconscious or dead and the aircraft
beginning to come apart—when both my energy and my hope
had drained away to nothingness—a mysterious voice came on
the radio and during a momentary break in the storm, guided
me into a safe landing on a snow-covered field. In that impossible
situation I had remembered God for the first time in 30-odd
years. I prayed fervently to him to save me and, most dramatically, he did.

A few days later, escaping from that stormy wintry scene,
I found myself in Mexico, coming into a Yoga academy in the

evening, just as the group of students assembled there were singing the arathi and waving a light in front of Swami's vibhuti-
covered picture. When I looked into the eyes of that image, I
choked up with tears. Suddenly something stirred most power-
fully in my dry heart. I didn't know who the picture was of and
why they left it covered with a heap of dust; but inwardly I
knew, unmistakably, that there was some powerful connection
between the voice that had come on the radio in that storm
over the Nevada desert and the holy man whose picture this
was. Soon I was told lots of wondrous stories of Baba and I said
to them, "O yes, I know all about him. He is the one who threw
the Chinese out of India on his birthday."

From that day on, I read everything of Baba that I could
lay my hands on; I went to Sai Centers and talked to devotees,
and I prepared myself in many ways to come into his presence.
Thus it was, about a year later, that I made my first pilgrimage
to Baba, reaching Prasanthi Nilayam during the Mahashivaratri
festival.

I was excited with anticipation, but also a little groggy from
jet-lag and the daze of suddenly landing in strange, noisy,
crowded India. At the ashram there was a huge throng over-
flowing the Poornachandra Auditorium. Our group had permission to be inside, so a phalanx of volunteers got behind us and
pushed; we landed in the auditorium with shouts of "Sai Ram!"
ringing out around us, as we stepped over people in a sudden
jostle.

I was in momentary confusion, and then seeing the massed
flags on the stage and the banners on the walls above, I went
into shock. It was as if I had suddenly been transported back
to an earlier phase of my existence. Here on the stage was
Swami's table, on which were inscribed two swastikas, an ancient
sacred symbol representing the OM; but for me this was the
terror-filled symbol of Nazi Germany where I had grown up as
a young boy and from which we had escaped with great difficulties just before the War. On the stage was a floral arch depicting
a gate on which was written "Work is Worship"; on the gates

of the concentration camps the Nazis had put a similar slogan, which roughly translated meant "Work Cleanses the Soul." The pageantry, the excitement of the crowd, the common greeting of Jai—which means the same thing as Heil—the adoration of the charismatic leader . . . all these sudden impressions created a most powerful feeling of deja vu.

Then I saw the SS carved in the base of Swami's chair, and I remembered an incident when I was nine years old. The situation for us had gotten so bad that I was sent off to live with relatives in Poland and to study there. I traveled alone by train across Germany. After a stop in Berlin, my well-to-do relations put me into a first-class compartment, not knowing that Jews were not permitted to travel by that class. At the next station there was a clatter of heels in the corridor outside and the door of my compartment flew open; a brown-uniformed soldier shouted "Achtung!" and a tall man—a dark eminence looking like death itself—strode into the compartment, straightened out his arm in the Nazi greeting and snapped out, "Heil Hitler!"

He was dressed in a black uniform with shiny knee-length black boots, a black belt across his chest, a black pistol holster on one side, a black dagger on the other side, a skull and crossbones on his peaked cap, a swastika band on his arm, a monocle perched in one eye, and white gloves covering his hands. He was holding a black riding crop.

Immediately I realized that a high officer of the dreaded SS, the action arm of the Gestapo, the secret police, had entered my life. For a moment I was petrified; I snapped to attention, took my bag and got ready to leave the compartment at once, when he said "Sit down!" I sat. He gave a quick look at his adjutant who was still by the door. The man clicked his heels in salute and closed the door.

The officer took off his hat, put away the monocle, took off the belt with its pistol and dagger, took off his gloves, put away the riding crop, loosened his collar and made himself comfortable.

He turned to me and said quite softly, "You're Jewish, I know. Well, boy, have you ever heard of Moses?"

I said, "Yes sir."

Then for the next hour he proceeded to tell me a number of Bible stories. My fear disappeared; I was fascinated and then I was charmed. He had a warm, soft voice and kind-looking eyes. He knew his Bible and he told the stories straight and sympathetically. Finally, he leaned very close to me and said, "Listen my boy, I like you. Let me give you some advice. This country has gone mad. Tell your parents to leave here as fast as you can. Don't stop until you are out of Europe, and don't worry about leaving your possessions. Just save your lives. This time there will be no Moses to lead you; you will have to do it yourself." In fact, we had applied for emigration to America, but the visas had been held up.

I was thinking of this when the train whistle blew, the shout of "Achtung!" was heard from outside the corridor. We were pulling into a station. The officer got up and put on all his paraphernalia. The door flew open to the same clicking of heels with which it had been closed. He turned to me, raised his hand in a stiff "Heil Hitler!" and then paused for just a moment at the door and gave me a knowing look. The last thing I remember seeing as he left the compartment were the two lightning strokes on each lapel of his uniform, signifying SS. Now as I sat in the Poornachandra that SS flashed back into my mind. The day I returned home a packet in the post brought the life-saving visas. We left on one of the last trains out of Germany.

Swami's discourse was over, and he started singing in that sweet, melodious voice of his that totally captivates the heart. I was catapulted back into the present; I remembered what I was doing there and why I had come on this journey. Here on stage was the ultimate of goodness—love personified—the divinity come with all its power and wisdom and glory into a human form, whose advent was of incalculable importance, something we have prayed for and waited for through countless lives. And long before we ever know of him, he works both within us and in the events around us. As in this story of the SS, it is only after coming to him that we begin to recognize his presence in all the critical situations that have occurred in our lives—one following the other like a succession of way-markers leading to him.

In the years that have gone by since that first trip to Swami, there have been countless personal experiences of his loving presence nurturing, guiding and correcting. If even a few hours go by in the day without feeling that direct, invisible but un-mistakable presence of Swami, I know that I've been uncon-scious.

He never rests, he never disappears, he never relaxes his vigilance; it is just these minds that get distracted and forget his sweet omnipresence. Everything and anything is possible for the divinity. Out of his unbounded love he will turn earth into heaven and heaven into earth for his devotees. He will come in countless forms and disguises and perform countless acts in order to rain surprise and delight and good lessons on us. We have all had many experiences and can tell Baba stories that would fill many books. The most wonderful realization is the connectedness of all the experiences—how they are like the un-foldment of scenes on an already existing tapestry, rendered in exquisite patterns, laced with surprising twists and twirls, and woven with immeasurable love by the master craftsman of them all. Everything taking place seems to have a genesis, a long his-tory in the past, which is then carefully guided into the present by the divine hand.

A few years after first coming to Swami, I had the notion of visiting an ashram in north India where some American friends were staying. In my mind there was a desire to listen to the discourses being given by their guru on the *Bhagavad Gita*. In darshan I asked Swami for permission to go there.

His reply was short and succinct, "One path. One teacher. No confusion. You stay." Clearly, I was not ready to go and listen to some other teacher. I stayed and put the trip completely out of my mind. A year later in darshan when I had totally forgotten about it, Swami said to me, "Now you can go to that place." But there had been many problems in that ashram and I no longer had any interest in going there. I asked Baba if I could go on a pilgrimage to the Ganges instead; he gave his consent. A few days later I was on my way to Delhi and then on to Rishikesh.

It was a long, hot, dusty, bouncy ride through one of the most-overcrowded parts of India. The heat, the stench, the teeming humanity, the lack of sanitary facilities along the way, all took their toll on this Western body. When I finally arrived in Rishikesh, the beautiful holy city at the foothills of the Himalayas where the Ganges becomes a mighty river running wide and strong, I was unable to appreciate any part of the visual beauty that was now all around me. I had become painfully ill with stomach cramps and fever.

I went to the office of the ashram where I had made my reservation, arriving there just as they were about to close for lunch. I asked the sadhu on duty for accommodations. He said there was no place in the ashram. Hadn't they received my letter and my telegram? No, nothing was received. Could he suggest some other place to try, perhaps a hotel or traveler's bungalow? No, there was no place available anywhere around. Could I leave my baggage there for a short time while I looked for a place? No, that would not be possible. Could I perhaps have a little drinking water? Sorry, it is already past closing time; there are tea shops around. And so, a few moments later I was out in the street in the Indian noon-time sun, sitting, or more correctly, slumping on my baggage, miserably sick and no place to go.

A nice looking young man came up to me and asked, "What is your native place?" It is one of the standard phrases Indians learn in school, and every foreigner who spends any extended time in India hears the query endless times, as children come up to practice their English. This time I couldn't handle it, I was feeling too miserable.

I said, "Please, go away."

He persisted, "But where did you come from?"

"From the south, from Andhra Pradesh, and I'm not well and I don't want to talk, so please leave me be."

But far from leaving me alone, the boy came closer and said, "Did you come from Sai Baba's ashram?"

I perked up. "Do you know of Sai Baba?" I asked.

"O yes!" he answered, "Baba told me to come here."

I said, "Then please do me a favor and get me some clean drinking water."

"I'll get it for you right away," he answered.

He walked a few steps away from me and suddenly he looked down at his hands; then he pivoted around and said, "Look, this has just come. It must be for you." His hand was filled with a nice big mound of white vibhuti, the kind that Swami makes.

Startled, I asked, "Where did it come from?"

"Well, I think it came through the air from Puttaparthi," he answered. I took the vibhuti from him and he went off to get me the glass of water. Just as I put a little bit in my mouth, the same sadhu that had seemed so unfriendly earlier, came running up to me flashing a big smile and said, "We have a room for you! One of the permanent residents will be off-station for some time. You can stay in his place. It's very nice. But now, come with me and wash up and have some lunch." He helped me with my baggage and showed me to the room. I could feel Swami's love flooding into me; I knew immediately that everything would be all right.

For days afterwards I wondered about the boy who had given me the vibhuti and had gone off to fetch me some water. I never saw him again, nor did anyone know of him. It is as if he had vanished into thin air.

I settled down in my luxurious room, complete with fan, shelves filled with books, closets, everything. At three in the morning I was awakened by the beautiful, heavenly sound of veena strummings. It went on without pause for many hours, coming from the room next door. Later in the day I had a chance to meet the old gentleman who lived in that room, who, as it turned out, had not stirred out of that room for 20 years. His whole life had become filled with the *Gita*, and he offered to instruct me in the deeper meaning of its verses.

For the next fortnight I became immersed in *Gita*. It was Swami's gift to satisfy a longing that had arisen a year earlier and that was to fructify still further years later, when I was blessed to be present as Swami gave his direct teaching of the *Bhagavad Gita* in the temple at Prasanthi Nilayam. In that way, he looks after us and guides us and takes care of us, and makes his presence constantly known to us, until we realize that there is no longer a separate entity feeling his presence. It becomes just like ice cream of two different flavors melting together on the tongue, until all there is is just the exquisite taste of the one sweetness, melting into the one joyous feeling of pure delight, pure goodness. That is Swami's love which becomes our love and soon envelopes our whole world.

● ● ●

Dearest Reader. Have I been able to give you some taste of the inner movement that takes place when Baba comes into our lives? Have you caught the flavor? Let me share one more incident with you. I was sitting on the veranda of the temple at Prasanthi Nilayam, lost within myself, when suddenly I opened my eyes and found Swami standing in front of me.

He said, "Drucker, what do you want?"

I replied, "Swamiji, I'm content, I'm satisfied."

"You mean you want nothing?" He asked.

"Swamiji, all I want is YOU." I said, putting my hands on my heart.

"That's not NOTHING," he rejoined. "That's EVERY-THING!" And he put his hand over mine on my heart and said, "Everything is here. Everything is here." Then he added, "And nothing is there," pointing out to the world.

I held his hand for a few seconds. I hardly registered the great wisdom contained in his words, I was so struck with his love. As if to punctuate the complete naturalness and connectedness of the moment, when he turned to speak to someone else sitting nearby, I noticed a spider entrapped in his hair. I reached up to take it out. He looked at me for a just a second and then continued his conversation with the other man, but at the same time he bent his head down ever so slightly to let me extricate the little thing, which was desperately tangled in the kinks and curls. Then, without turning his head, he said to me, "Be careful, it may be a scorpion. It may sting." But it came out quite peacefully and there was no sting.

In this way life goes on at the ashram of the Lord, life that is heart to heart, bathed in the continuous presence of the ever-loving mother, the stern father, delightful friend, divine teacher, beloved Self.

Let me conclude with a personal note. For seven years following that first journey to India, I made twice-yearly pilgrimages from America to the lotus feet. On one of those trips, Swami told me to stop doing individual healing work and, instead, to teach. With Swami's blessing a school of alternative medicine and healing came up at our institute and became very popular among health professionals and lay people interested in holistic health. Just as we were at the height of success, Swami told me in an interview on a trip in early 1981, "Close everything up and leave it. Come be with Swami." And then he gave a little poem, which has stuck with me like a mantra. He said, "You don't need marriage, you don't need money and you don't need fame—all of those will lead to pain." He was speaking of the three goals of worldly life, the purusharthas as they are called in India. Leave them behind and put everything into reaching the fourth, be free, be with me.

I came back to America, terminated my affairs there and within a month left to settle in India. But now, years later, I realize that Swami was not referring to an outer change of residence but an inner transformation. And that doesn't come quite as quickly as buying an airplane ticket and getting rid of a few possessions. After a second round of seven years, that process has hardly begun. During these years there have been many experiences of his beneficent grace but there have also been many bumps and jumps.

All of this is another chapter; and, dear reader, I have already kept you too long. In parting, again I salute you with my love and best wishes, that you may receive all blessings, and realize the blissful Lord who is your own immortal self.

Ideas, principles, laws, codes, habits, actions—all are to be judged on the twin points of intention and consequence. Is the intention pure, is it born out of Love? Is it based on Truth? Does it result in Peace? If yes, Dharma is enshrined in that action or law, custom or conduct.

—Sathya Sai Baba

UNITY IS DIVINITY

Mary Lynn Radford

Part One
Lynn, Bal Vikas Child

When I think of our daughter, Lynn, a mosaic of bright images comes to mind; Lynn, the child of whimsy, improvisor of games and stories which delighted her friends. As one of them would later say, "Wherever Lynn was, there was laughter." Lynn, the true Bal Vikas who loved to show reverence for her parents, serving me breakfast on Mother's Day and tenderly caring for her father as he recovered from surgery. Lynn, the honor student, who loved school. Lynn, the child who at 14 when other girls her age talked about boys, preferred to sing bhajans and yes, climb trees. And most of all, a Lynn who loved Baba with a devotion which would awaken an introspective quality in her and a desire for solitude in which to write poems and thoughts of Baba in her diary. Indeed, her intensity of devotion would draw her two younger brothers and her parents closer to God.

It was in the winter of 1974 that I prayed for holy company. I know now it was Baba who answered my prayer; for, soon afterwards, through a dear friend, we learned about him, and Lynn and I began going to bhajans at our Santa Barbara Sai Baba Center.

It was Lynn who, after seeing our first Baba film at the center said, "Mommy, we must have our own meditation corner." She promptly removed all the books from a recessed book case in our back hall, and thenceforth it was our altar where we meditated daily.

My hopes and unspoken prayers for the children's spiritual education were quickly answered by Baba when, shortly after joining the Sai family, our head of center formed a Bal Vikas class. Thus, at Thursday evening bhajans and again on Sunday at Bal Vikas class, Lynn's devotion had precious opportunities to grow and flower.

Indeed, she was the only child present at the daily celebration of Dasara and was proud and happy when asked to participate in the reading of the Chandi. On the culminating evening of Dasara that fall of 1975, I remember seeing tears of joy in Lynn's eyes as she offered a flower to the Mother. And at Shivaratri some four months later, while many adults were too tired to continue, Lynn's ardor sustained her (as it had the previous year) through the night-long vigil of meditation, prayer and bhajan.

At times like these my pride in her devotion was tempered by occasional thoughts that perhaps her zeal was abnormal for a child her age. Little did I realize that Lynn was being guided tenderly by our Lord and prepared for the culmination of her short life.

It was Thursday afternoon, ten days before Easter, the all important date on the Christian calendar which commemorates the resurrection of Jesus Christ. School had finished for the day. Lynn had gone to the park, and I knew she was heading for the tall pine, her favorite climbing tree. I remember watching from the kitchen window as she darted off, calling in her sweet voice for our dog, Jupiter, to follow.

Only 45 minutes later a neighbor came to tell me that Lynn had had a fall. In her haste to help her brother David, who had been bitten by a strange dog and was crying, she had stepped on a broken branch and fallen some twelve feet to the ground.

As I ran I heard Lynn call, "Mommy, Mommy!" And as I reached her side, she seemed to know I was with her. She lay quietly and did not seem to be in pain; thus I had no idea she was so near death. I prayed earnestly as I held her hand, "Baba, please be with Lynn, please be with Lynn . . ." An hour later, in the Catholic hospital nearby, a priest was administering the last rites as she quietly passed on.

Numb with grief, I asked Baba for reassurance. The first thought that came was: "Why, it is Thursday, Baba's day." Indeed, two short hours after Lynn's passing, bhajans and prayers of our Santa Barbara center were lifting her spirit.

That night I could not sleep. I was tormented by the knowledge that Lynn, stunned by her fall, had perhaps been unable to think of Baba at the time of her going. The next morning when I went to her room, Baba had already answered my anguish. There on Lynn's desk were her last words, written just before going to the park. They were a fateful synthesis of the morning and evening prayers:

"O, Lord, I rise now from the womb of slumber. Before I plunge again into the daily routine, let me pray most earnestly to Thee, omniscient Self, and seek thy lap, which confers on me restful sleep and blesses me with eternal peace and everlasting bliss."

Our minister was so struck by this event that he opened the memorial service for Lynn with these very words.

The prayer had been written in her favorite purple ink, ready to be inserted into the new Bal Vikas notebook, which her teacher had provided the day before her death. The notebook was to be a replacement for the one David had lost on the way to Sunday morning Omkar at the center two weeks previously. Now I know why David had lost the notebook. It was all part of Baba's design. At the time I had marveled at Lynn. She did not get angry at David. She had simply said, "Well, Mommy, since our center leader is moving to a new house, I shall start a new notebook." I told her how happy I was that she did not get angry with David. "You see how Baba is answering your prayers," I said. She had often asked Baba for help in dealing with, as I told her, very natural feelings of sibling rivalry with her younger brother. But Lynn, ever the perfectionist, had been upset by her occasional negative feelings toward him, and she had often prayed to Baba for help. That's why I now know that the way Lynn died was also part of Baba's design: she had fallen in the act of hurrying to David's rescue; her last act was a selfless one.

It became clear that Lynn's death was no "accident" but, like her life, another part of Baba's tapestry. In the days to follow, other parts of the pattern would fall into place, revealing to me as I had never experienced it before, that Baba's loving network was indeed the basis of all existence.

The following day, a dear friend who is a long-standing devotee of Baba, brought us an inspiring message. After bhajans, having learned of Lynn's death, she had gone into deep meditation in an effort to "find" Lynn. She reported experiencing great light, a lifting as on angels' wings, and overwhelming joy. Any shreds of my doubts were swept away, and we wept together.

And then, a crowning touch: late Saturday we learned that Mr. Vimu Mukunda, distinguished musician from Bangalore, India, and former atomic scientist, who was now a kind of spiritual troubadour for Baba, had just "happened" to be visiting friends near Santa Barbara when news came of Lynn's passing. He wished to play the veena at Lynn's memorial service.

The morning of Lynn's service, Palm Sunday (one week before Easter), dawned fair and sunny after a brief shower of rain which seemed like a touch of grace. Well do I remember the tangible aura of peace in Lynn's room that day. Later, after the service, friends would remark on it with a sense of awe.

The service was a beautiful one consisting of prayers, readings from the Bible and the *Bhagavad Gita*, and Lynn's own poems. And the high point was Mr. Mukunda's veena solo which he concluded by leading us all in singing Lynn's favorite bhajan, "Jai Durga, Lakshmi, Saraswati . . ."

How grateful I was to Baba for Mr. Mukunda's presence. It was as if the Lord had blessed the event to be one of celebration rather than lament.

After the service, friends who did not know of Baba came up to us with grief in their faces. How could I tell them—and yet our friends in the Baba family understood—that our daughter had been blessed in her short life to come to Baba in her heart, to love this avatar, who had now raised her pure spirit to him. The tears in my eyes that day were tears of joy and reverence. Only much later would our emotions catch up with us, and acknowledge the finality of Lynn's going.

Shortly after this, a friend and adopted grandmother added another image to Baba's tapestry. Three weeks before Lynn's passing, during a special function at our center, we had seen inspiring films of India; and on the way home that night Lynn had asked her, "When do you think I shall go to see Baba? I want to so much."

That very night, our friend told me, she had had a dream in which Baba came to her saying, "In 21 days she will come to me." At that time our friend was in very poor health and she thought Baba meant that she was to die in three weeks. Then, after Lynn's death, she realized that Baba must have been referring to Lynn in the dream, because it was 21 days after that Lynn fell from the tree.

As our head of center remarked, everyone in our Sai family was deeply affected by the love Lynn left behind; a love she had quietly and undemonstratively shared as a participant in our worship. Her going made each of us re-evaluate ourselves and understand how vital each individual is to the life of a center.

And finally, as a legacy of Lynn's passing, her father, who had been an atheist, became a spiritual seeker. The poetry of paradox was again revealed. We usually consider death a tragic event; yet in this instance, as a dear friend would say, Lynn's life and death were a beautiful solo in Baba's symphony. Indeed, Baba sent my husband a vivid dream which pointed out to him that our child had given him the key to a priceless treasure, awareness of divinity within. Some months later he would share with me, "Lynn has given me a gift—I am now a believer."

I will close with our daughter's own words which she wrote on a family camping trip:

The golden sun climbs up from behind
A round, green hill.
All the sky is blue, cold and open.
Sai Baba stands on a single rock,
Smiling with the glory of dawn.

And this poem, expressing her yearning, which our minister shared at her memorial service:

> *To Baba, who sits on a golden throne;*
> *Surrounded by snowflakes and frothy sea foam.*
> *Come into my heart*
> *Remove with your touch the tears of my heart*
> *And replace them with a blissful song . . .*

Part Two
Why Fear When I Am Here?

Shortly after Lynn's story appeared in the *Sanathana Sarathi*, I found myself in a period of depression. Perhaps the sharing of our daughter's story stirred up some residue of grief, or perhaps it was simply one of those dry spells that occur from time to time in the devotee's life. Whatever the reason, I found myself praying to Baba for a special sign of his love. I did not specify what it should be; I simply asked him for reassurance.

One week later, my prayer was answered in a most dramatic way. Coming to bhajans that Sunday evening I was surprised to see Mr. Vimu Mukunda, distinguished devotee of Baba and talented musician, who had actually played his veena at Lynn's memorial service three years earlier. We had not seen him in all this time, for he had been traveling around the world. After our bhajans, the center president asked Mr. Mukunda to share Baba's words about Lynn.

As she was introducing him, I could scarcely believe what was happening. Had Baba heard my plea? I listened as Mr. Mukunda revealed that he had just happened to be in Baba's presence when Mr. Kasturi, according to his custom, was asking Baba's permission to publish the stories slated to appear in the March, 1979, issue. Among them was the story of Lynn which

I had submitted to him. Mr. Kasturi then asked Baba about Lynn, and Mr. Mukunda heard Baba say: "She was a beautiful child who brought joy to all who knew her. Why hold her back? She has finished her karma. She is with me."

Tears of joy filled my eyes as I listened to Mr. Mukunda speak. Although at the time of Lynn's passing many miraculous signs reassured us that she had indeed "graduated" from this university of the world, here was the proof of her liberation from Baba's own lips, coming to me as if in direct answer to my prayer for a special sign.

As I look back, I now realize that this dramatic incident prepared the way for my first journey to India to see Swami's physical form, a journey which would materialize a year later; and the process of transformation hastened by our daughter's death would continue.

During this first visit in Brindavan, Baba would take me through the ABC's of spirituality, starting with his first commandment, the basis for all spiritual evolution: "God is one"; or, in Swami's words: "Unity is Divinity."

Now at this point in my life I certainly loved God and my fellow man; I had worked hard to implement Baba's teachings, and I was quite sincere when I told him mentally just prior to the trip: I desire nothing from you Baba; I do not need miraculous manifestations of vibhuti and the like. I wish only to experience your divine love and to share it.

Our longed-for interview with Baba would take place. Baba manifested vibhuti for a sick child, her mother weeping tears of gratitude. He asked most people in the group, "What do you want?" But when it was my turn, he asked gently, "And how are you?"

"I'm happy Baba. Very happy," I replied.

"Happy, very happy," he said sweetly. And I felt a wave of bliss flooding my entire being.

That was all; then he went on around the group, and when it was my friend's turn, he asked, "And what do you want?"

She replied, "Baba, I want to know if you are the Godhead."

Baba answered, "Who is God? What is God? You must experience."

My friend asked, "Will you help me?"

"Yes, yes, I will help," he replied, and then he made the familiar circular motion and manifested vibhuti for her, which he proceeded to share with some in the group. He skipped over me, however; later I realized that he had honored my intent: hadn't I told him that I desired no physical manifestations?

Baba then went into a discourse with my friend about her "monkey mind" and reminded her that she must "choose" spirituality. Finally, he said, "Do you want Sai Baba?" and when she said, "Yes," he manifested a ring for her. The ring was large and showed Swami with his right hand raised in the familiar mudra of reassurance to his devotees.

At this point my own monkey mind took over, and I felt a sense of dismay. I very quickly forgot my noble intentions and thought: I wish he would manifest a japamala for me! No sooner had this thought crossed my mind when Baba actually materialized one and dangled it enticingly in front of us, swinging it back and forth like a pendulum! Would he give it to me? With a twinkle in his eye, Baba tossed it to a devotee from Italy, a stocky lady already sporting a huge ring which Baba had given her on a previous visit. I couldn't believe it. From there on, it was all down hill. By the time the interview was over my mind was making the mad monkey look like a sage by comparison.

The next day I found myself looking into that Pandora's box which Baba had opened. What I saw didn't please me one bit: jealousy, unworthiness, self pity, and so it went. Where were all those "divine" feelings I had been so sure I would experience? The day following this encounter with my supposedly non-existent ego, I finally came to my senses.

"Baba, what am I doing? I came here to ask of you only one thing: Please take all this petty egoism, and let me be a channel for your divine love."

And this time I really meant it; it was not just a pious wish. As I waited in the darshan line that morning, tears filled my eyes, and I held up my japamala. Baba seemed to know what was in my heart for he walked over to me directly and put his hand firmly on my japamala, blessing it and filling my heart with joy. Gone was the anguish and doubt of the day before. I was transformed.

It was as if he were saying: "Now that you are willing to surrender the self-image which was so precious, I can give you what I wanted to give you all along: the experience of your own divinity." That day, for the first time in my life I know I actually experienced divine love; I felt as though I were floating six inches above the ground.

The days of our first visit were flying rapidly by. On the 19th of January (we had arrived on the 4th) Baba was due to leave for Madras and then for Bombay. We were slated to leave for the states on the 21st; but there was no way to know Baba's timetable. We decided to see the travel agent to confirm our seats on the 7:30 P.M. flight, which wasn't due to arrive until 9:00 P.M. on the 21st. That would give us ample time to make the midnight Air India connection in Bombay. The travel agent hesitated: "I think you had better get the noon flight to insure plenty of time to make the connection." My friend and I looked at each other. It occurred to us simultaneously: this was a sign that we might be seeing Baba in Bombay after all.

Meanwhile, the theme of oneness continued to assert itself during our visit. On the morning of the 19th before Baba was due to leave for Madras, unknown to one another, each of us had been inspired with the idea of presenting Baba flowers during morning darshan. This would be our last contact with him and a way of expressing our love and gratitude; however, as it would turn out, neither of us did buy any from the flower sellers that morning. No sooner had we walked into the darshan area when a friend, whom we had met at the ashram, approached us holding not one, but two garlands. She said that Baba had appeared in her morning meditation and told her that our love was a magnet; he wanted each of us to have flowers! And, of course, as events unfolded, Baba did stop to bless each of our garlands that morning as we held them up for a last goodbye.

The next night, our last in Bangalore before departure, we were invited to the home of Kekie Mistry, official photographer for Baba. We felt it was another farewell gift from Baba as Kekie treated us to slides of the recent birthday celebration and World Conference at Prasanthi Nilayam. This was especially meaningful for us because Baba had remained at Brindavan during our entire visit, and so we had not had the opportunity to make the trip to Puttaparthi.

During the evening my friend was inspired to purchase one of Kekie's photographs. This particular photo, Kekie told us, was one of Baba's favorites—Swami had told him, "This is the face of God." And so I followed suit. Suppose we did have the chance to see Baba in Bombay, and suppose he were to autograph them for us? An extravagant wish, given the unpredictability of Baba's travel itinerary; but by then we were both learning that miracles are the order of the day in a devotee's life. It's simply a matter of staying awake.

In the Dharmakshetra, unlike Brindavan where there were a few hundred devotees at most, there were thousands waiting for a glimpse of Baba. Our hearts sank; how could we even hope for contact with him? We sought out a volunteer and explained that this would be our last opportunity for Baba's darshan as we would be departing that evening for the States. Kindly enough she seated us somewhere towards the center of the vast throng and disappeared. But a few moments later, for no apparent reason, she reappeared and directed us to follow her. This time she took us to the front of the crowd and seated us, like V.I.P.'s, in the first row behind the bhajan leaders. Further, she seated me right on the aisle, so that if Baba came near, I would have an opportunity to hold up the photograph.

Well, you guessed it. Baba did come to me and sign my photograph, "Love, Baba" as my friend and I had prayed he would. We had agreed that if Baba should sign my photograph,

I would then hold up hers, but when I did so, Baba shook his head and murmured gently, "Only one."

For just a few moments it was my friend's turn to feel left out; and then the true meaning of Baba's actions dawned on us both. As we discussed it later on our trip home, we realized that Baba's words, "Only one," had been the theme of our entire trip; the precious lesson he had given us. And he had provided opportunities for each of us to confront our self-created obstacles to that awareness—for instance, my experience in the interview. Having provoked these happenings, he had then given us dramatic glimpses of our oneness; for example, that morning when our Seattle friend gave us the garlands; the insight we shared in the travel agent's office; and the realization that had it not been for her impulse to buy the photo of Baba at the slide party, and had she not provided the pen which Baba used to sign it, I would not now have this treasured sign of his love on my altar.

What does oneness mean? Baba gives us a practical test. When we feel pain at another's pain, and more difficult, joy at another's joy, then we can know that we are experiencing the divine unity he speaks of.

As if to underscore the significance Baba attaches to this teaching, an event happened several years after my trip to prove to both my husband and myself that we had finally "internalized" this principle.

I was gathering notes and remembering the highlights of that first trip to Baba, preparing for a talk on "Unity is Divinity" at a neighboring Sai center, when out of the blue, my brother-in-law came to visit. He had driven all the way from Los Angeles to share startling news. After years of setbacks in business (which had involved considerable financial sacrifice on my husband's part in order to help his brother), Peter announced that his ship had come in. A major chemical company was about to produce and distribute his invention, and so bright were the prospects, it now seemed that he would be a millionaire in two years time.

Our spontaneous reaction to this sudden news was one of pure joy. For both my husband and myself there was not even a hint of the "if-only-it-had-happened-to-us" syndrome; simply genuine happiness that Peter and his family would be enjoying the kind of life-style they had long hoped for.

And then I experienced a flashback—I was recalling my very different reaction during our interview five years ago, at my friend's grace in receiving a ring from Baba. At that time I had felt contraction and dismay, but now, on hearing Peter's news, I was experiencing a sense of expansion and joy at his good fortune; and this in spite of the strained relationship which had grown up between our two families. I knew now that the timing of Peter's visit was Baba's. He had given us the opportunity to realize that we were progressing on the path.

After Peter left, I felt joy at having passed Baba's surprise "quiz," and perhaps it was the catalyst for what happened next. I had resumed preparing notes for the talk on unity, and was recalling my experience in the interview with Baba when the revelation occurred.

In the interview room Baba had asked me, "And how are you?" I had replied, "I am happy Baba, very happy." Then he had said, "Happy, very happy." At that instant a wave of bliss had surged up within me, and now I realized the bliss I had felt was also his: He and I were one. Implicit in that moment of ecstasy was the knowing, the experience of divine union. And I had been foolish enough to regret not being given a japamala.

This incident was for me a graphic example of how Baba's time-frame differs from our own. Lovingly he had saved for me the "fruits" of my lesson on unity until, in the fullness of my own time, I was able to demonstrate that I had grasped the principle.

It is typical of Baba in his role as teacher of his devotees to validate learning in this new way. As he has assured us, there are no shortcuts on the spiritual path. Only by manifesting in our lives and in our awareness the love and unity he teaches, can each of us claim the divinity within. As the *Course in*

Miracles states: "To give and to receive are one. To know love, teach love." Or in the words of Saint Francis of Assisi, "It is in giving that we receive."

In my case he had first prepared me for the experience of unity by putting me in touch with my feelings of separateness and the resulting doubts and fears which, until his merciful intervention, had been blocking my awareness of my true nature—for how many lifetimes?

For most of us in Baba's orbit, synchronous events and happenings—"chance" meetings and the like—gradually prepare us for the experience of unity which he speaks of. I like to call these events "cosmic coincidence;" and over and over again in the charmed life of the devotee, Baba uses these little miracles to remind us that we are one with our fellow beings and one with him.

They will often occur in a moment of crisis when we are thinking of him. At such times he lifts the veil of maya—or what we in the West might simply refer to as the world being too much with us; when pressing concerns can blind us to the larger reality.

Recently my older son experienced an emotional breakdown. He had moved to a neighboring county. I was not acquainted with any psychologists or support services, and I was at a loss and floundering. I asked Baba for guidance; and the very first thought that occurred was to call a devotee in this nearby community whose son had experienced similar difficulties; and so I placed the call.

She could not recommend a specific psychiatrist but suggested that I call a psychologist who had worked with her son in the past. As matters developed, this young man responded to my call in such a way that I knew Baba was guiding me step by step. He told me he was about to have lunch with his best friend who just happened to be a psychiatrist and the head of the county's Continuing Care Services. This man, he assured me, was a highly spiritual person and one he would recommend for my son.

To make a long story short, a week later we walked into this psychiatrist's office for my son's first visit. And what should we see on his bookshelf but a copy of the *Course in Miracles*. I found myself thinking, "Thank you, Baba; obviously, this man is a seeker."

But the crowning touch was yet to come. As the psychiatrist began talking with my son, I noticed four copies of a book right on his desk in front of him. I took a closer look. It was none other than the beautiful *Supremacy of God* by Ilon—a series of vedantic essays which constitute a hymn of praise to Sai Baba as avatar of the age. This particular book, as it happened, was the one my younger son had given to his Bal Vikas teacher as a Christmas gift!

Not only had we been guided to a doctor who could identify with my son's devotion to Baba, but also he was a total vegetarian and, in fact, he had just finished reading Dr. Samuel Sandweiss's book *Spirit and the Mind*.

Needless to say, it was one of those "Why fear when I am here?" episodes so dear to the heart of the devotee; the synchronicity which is our proof ongoing, of the eternal bond linking each of us with him.

As I look back over my life, it becomes increasingly clear that only those experiences which have inspired love and awareness of unity have any meaning. The downers, difficulties, losses and trials I now perceive as unique opportunities which Baba seized upon to awaken me.

So, indeed, what is good? What is bad? Most often what the world considers "good" has the effect of prolonging the delusion; while the "bad" removes it. As devotees we are supremely blessed in knowing that by turning to Baba we can experience the truth of this cosmic paradox, and we are thus empowered to weave whole cloth out of the warp and woof, the seeming ups and downs of our lives.

More and more, life in this world appears to be a gigantic "koan," unsolvable by the mind; solvable, in fact, only by love.

Has he not assured us: *"It is the heart that reaches the goal. Follow the heart! A pure heart seeks beyond the intellect. It gets inspired."*

This is the transformation Baba brings about in each of us. He is our divine psychotherapist, slowly, gently and surely removing the blocks to love's awareness.

I am always with you, even if you don't believe in me, even when you try to forget me, even when you laugh at me or hate me, even when I seem to be on the opposite side of the earth. I am in you. You are in me. Don't forget that. We cannot be separated!

—Sathya Sai Baba

GLOSSARY

Amrit: Nectar, symbolizing immortality.

Arati: The worshipping of God with the flame of camphor. The flame represents the burning of all desires.

Arjuna: White, pure, unblemished, unsullied; Arjuna was one of the Pandava brothers and the hero of the Bhagavad Gita.

Ashram: A spiritual community.

Atma: The spark of God within, the soul.

Avatar: An incarnation of God; descent of God on earth in human form.

Bal Vikas: The educational wing of the Sathya Sai Baba Organization whose goal is to foster spiritual development in children and to teach them the basic human values: Truth, Right Action, Peace, Love and Nonviolence. Literal meaning "blossoming of the child."

Bhagavad Gita: The Song of God, a major Indian scripture.

Bhajan: Devotional singing.

Brindavan: The place where Sai Baba's school and ashram is located, near Bangalore. Brindavan symbolizes the pure heart of the devotee where the Lord plays in joy.

Chandi: A sacred book of the Hindus, read during Durga puja; describing the Divine Mother's destruction of the demons.

Darshan: Seeing a holy person; to see the form of the Lord and receive his blessings.

Dasara: The festival that celebrates the victory of the forces of good over the forces that resist the progress of humanity toward light.

Dharma: The dictates of God, the duty of man, code of conduct or self-disciplinary rules, duty, obligation, codes of morality, righteousness.

Dharmakshetra: The abode of righteousness, purified area of virtue; the name of the temple for Sai Baba in Bombay.

Dhoti: The loincloth worn by Hindu men.

Dovening: In Judaism, praying, sometimes accompanied by a rocking motion.

Ganesha: The remover of obstacles; the elephant-faced son of Lord Shiva.

Gayatri Mantra: Sacred chant that both protects and illumines the minds of those who recite it.

Guru: Teacher, dispeller of darkness.

Hatha Yoga: School of Yoga which emphasizes union with God through asanas (physical postures).

Jai: Victory.

Japa: Continual repetition of the name of the Lord.

Japamala: 108 beads used in the repetition of the name of God; similar to a rosary.

Jnana Yoga: The path of wisdom; the possession of this knowledge enables you to experience the unity of all life.

Kaddish: A prayer in praise of God by mourners after death of a relative.

Kali: The name for the divine Mother, the primal energy.

Karma: Action; an inescapable obligation or duty that has to be performed due to past deeds.

Karma Yoga: Performing all action and dedicating it to God.

Krishna: Lord Krishna. An avatar who lived about 5000 years ago.

Lingam: Symbol of creation, symbolizes the form of God, as in the Shivalingam, the merging of the form with the formless. Because of the oval shape of the lingam, there is no beginning or ending, so it merges with the formless.

Lotus feet: Refers to the feet of the Lord.

Maha Shivarathri: *See* Shivarathri.

Mandir: Temple.

Mantra: Chant, sacred words.

Maya: Ignorance obscuring the vision of God; the primary illusion is the world.

Mudra: Pose of the hand conveying a specific meaning.

Namama: "Thy Will is my Will."

OM: The original, the first sound of the supreme universal reality called Brahman; the most sacred word of the vedas.

Omkar: Repetition of OM. Omkar is recited 21 times at the ashram before dawn.

Padnamaskar: Touching the feet with devotion, which symbolizes surrender to the Lord.

Poornachandra: A large auditorium at Sai Baba's ashram that holds over 20,000 people.

Prasanthi Nilayam: Name of Baba's ashram, meaning "Abode of the Higest Peace."

Premaswarupa: Term of endearment used by Baba meaning "embodiments of love."

Puja: Worship, in a prescribed manner.

Purusharthas: The four goals of life.

Puttaparthi: Name of village in India where Baba was born and where his ashram is now located.

Rajasic: The active, passionate aspect of nature.

Sadhu: A holy man, generally used with reference to a monk.

Sai Ram: Name for Sai Baba. This avatar now known as Sai Baba incarnated in ancient times as Rama. "Sai Ram" is a greeting used by Baba's devotees.

Sanathana Sarathi: "The Eternal Charioteer," name of the monthly publication from Prasanthi Nilayam.

Sari(s): Indian woman's traditional dress.

Sarva Dharma: Acknowledgement of all religions.

Satsang: Spending time in the company of others on the spiritual path.

Seva dal: Service workers.

Shanti: Eternal Peace.

Shma Yisrael, Adaunoi Elauhenu, Adaunoi Echod: means "Hear O Israel, the Lord our God, the Lord is One."

Shirdi Baba: A great Indian saint. Previous incarnation of Sai Baba.

Sivarathri: Literally, "the night of Siva." A time of austerity and intensified spiritual practice on that night in the Lunar calendar when the moon is smallest and furthest from the earth, therefore enabling spiritual aspirants to steady their minds and achieve liberation.

Shul: Synagogue.

Sloka: Verse form of the Sanskrit epics.

Soham: Means "I am He," signifying the identity of the individual soul with God.

Swami: Lord, master, spiritual preceptor.

Tallith, Tallithim: A tassled prayer shawl worn by orthodox Jews.

Tapas: Disciplined spiritual practices to control and coordinate the functions of the body, austerity.

Vedanta: Philosophy originating in India that teaches the ultimate knowledge, such as "All is One."

Vedas: Sacred scriptures of the Hindus.

Veena: Indian stringed musical instrument.

Vibhuti: Holy ash with curative powers, frequently materialized by Sai Baba.

Whitefield: A town outside of Bangalore where Baba has established a boys' college as well as a smaller ashram.

Yarmulke: A skull cap worn by orthodox Jews.

Yogis: Contented God-centered men; those who are given to simple living and who practice the disciplines, physical and mental, of yoga.

BIBLIOGRAPHY

A *Course in Miracles*. Tiburon, CA: Foundation for Inner Peace, 1975.

de Nicolas, Antonio, tr. *Bhagavad Gita*. York Beach, ME: Nicolas-Hays, 1990.

Fanibunda, Eruch B. *Vision of the Divine*. Bombay: E.B. Fanibunda, 1977.

Hilsop, John. *Conversations with Sathya Sai Baba*. San Diego, CA: Birth Day Publishing, 1978.

_____. *My Baba and I*. San Diego, CA: Birth Day Publishing, 1985.

Ilon, *The Supremacy of God*. San Diego, CA: Birth Day Publishing, 1980.

Murphet, Howard. *Sai Baba Avatar*. San Diego, CA: Birth Day Publishing, 1977.

_____. *Sai Baba—Man of Miracles*. York Beach, ME: Samuel Weiser, 1973.

Kasturi, N. *Sathya Sai Speaks, Volumes 1-11*, Discourses from 1953-1982. Sri Sathya Books and Publications, 1962. Prasanthi Nilayam, Anantapur District, A.P., India 515134

_____. *Sathyam, Shivam, Sundaram*. Four volume biography. Bangalore, India: Sri Sathya Sai Publications and Education Foundation. Vol. 1, 1960; Vol. 2, 1968; Vol. 3, 1972; Vol. 4, 1980.

Krystal, Phyllis. *Sai Baba—The Ultimate Experience*. Los Angeles: Aura Books, 1985.

Sandweiss, Samuel H. *Sai Baba: The Holy Man . . . And the Psychiatrist*. San Diego, CA: Birth Day Publishing, 1975.

_____. *Spirit and the Mind*. San Diego, CA: Birth Day Publishing, 1985.

For more information on Sathya Sai Baba, and to order copies of Kasturi's works, write to:

> Sathya Sai Book Center of America
> 305 West First Street
> Tustin, California 92680

Your own heart shining with Love is God's Love. You are God.
The true you is God.

—Sathya Sai Baba